POSTHUMAN *LEAR*

Figure 1. Hieronymus Bosch, *Ship of Fools* (1490–1500).

First published in 2016 by punctum books, Earth, Milky Way.
www. punctumbooks.com

ISBN-13: 978-0692641576
ISBN-10: 0692641572
Library of Congress Cataloging Data is available from the Library of Congress

Cover image: Sophia Schorr-Kon, *Delphine's Call,* 2012. Courtesy of the artist. Sophia Schorr-Kon explores the wide and dynamic range of human emotion through her lens. Referencing contemporary culture, her personal experiences and art history as her visual terminology, her aim is to reach into the depths of what it is to be human, to love and to lose, to rise and fall, and to unearth, distill, and express the wisdom and beauty that can be found in all of our natural states of being.
To find more of her work, visit http://www.sophiaschorr-kon.com

Copy editing: Kristen McCants
Book design: Vincent W.J. van Gerven Oei

No sheep were killed in the making of this book.

Craig Dionne:

HIS
Posthuman LEAR:
Reading Shakespeare in the Anthropocene

Approaching King Lear *from an eco-materialist*
perspective, examining how the shift in
SHAKESPEARE's tragedy from court
to stormy heath activates a different
sense of language as tool-being
—from that of participating
in the flourish of aristocratic
prodigality & circumstance,
to that of survival and
pondering one's
interdependence
with a denuded
world.

❧

Earth, Milky Way,
Printed for *punctum books,* and are to be sold at shops
all around the world at the sign of the typewriter key *P*
2016

Praise the world to the angel, not what can't be talked about.
You can't impress him with your grand emotions. In the cosmos
Where he so intensely feels, you're just a novice. So show
Him some simple thing shaped for generation after generation
Until it lives in our hands and in our eyes, and it's ours.
Tell him about things. He'll stand amazed, just as you did
Beside the ropemaker in Rome or the potter on the Nile.
Show him how happy a thing can be, how innocent and ours.

— Rainer Maria Rilke, *Duino Elegies*

Ex arena funiculum nectis
You are twisting a rope of sand
To twist a rope of sand. This means trying in vain to do what
can by no means be done. What could be sillier than to twist a
rope out of sand, which cannot stick together? ... The proverb
can be particularly adapted to use as follows: if one should try
to bring into agreement people who are far apart in way of
life, with whatever in common; or if one should put together
speech woven out of discordant arguments, creating a kind
of chimera or a monster like that described by Horace, with
a man's head on a horse's neck and with the rest of limbs collected from kinds of animals...

— Erasmus, *Adagia*

In Memory

Teoman Sipahigil

1939–2014

I'm referring to the text, Teo.

CONTENTS

ACKNOWLEDGMENTS

This book was written while on sabbatical in Tokyo, Japan, June 2014 to June 2015. Many hands helped to make this institutional support possible: Eastern Michigan University's research support—especially that of my department's unflagging Research and Sabbatical Leave Committee, our department head Mary Ramsey (her "leave the chalk, take the cannolis" attitude made this workable), and Kim Schatzel, EMU's Provost, and Tom Venner, Arts and Sciences Dean. I also need to thank Arata Ide and Keio University in Tokyo for sponsoring my application for a Visiting Researcher position. The librarians at Keio's Mita Campus Media Library were very helpful and gracious with my errant questions, especially Hijiri Okamoto. The book grew out of many lively interactions with students and colleagues about posthuman theory, speculative realism, and animal studies in my department's reading group, and with scholarship in Shakespeare and early modern English literature, specifically through workshops and panels at Shakespeare Association of America and BABEL. Steve Mentz, Sharon O'Dair, Laura George, and Natasa Kovacevic offered patience, careful advice, and thoughtful suggestions. Christine Neufeld helped me with careful copyediting. Ruth Evans helped with obvious drafts, and included an earlier chunk of the project on the Modern Language Association special New Materialisms panel (Vancouver, BC 2015). Eileen Joy, too, can be credited with perusing the bulk of earlier drafts and encouraging publication. For students of the Renaissance, it becomes clear that humanism was the product of the singular stamina, table cheer, and long distance friendships fostered by amazing people like Desiderius Erasmus. And I often think of Eileen Joy as the Erasmus of today's humanities; her remarkable energy is an exemplar in these uncertain, exciting times. I also want to acknowledge students with whom I have shared many ideas, especially Nathan Kelber, Elizabeth Dieterich, Abdulhamit Arvas, Evan Lee, Michael Shumway, and Martin Goffeney. Special thanks to Sophia Schorr-Kon and Hatsuki Nishio for letting me use their photography. The readers at punctum books put much energy into my manuscript; their careful suggestions were extremely useful and encouraging. Also at punctum books, Kristen McCants and Vincent van Gerven Oei helped tremendously with getting the book into shape. My wife Shay and my sons Brenan and Carter were always there when I needed to walk away from the page. In their own way they made the uncertainty of the writing process livable while on sabbatical. Everyone listed here made this worth writing.

This is the Thing

You shall see, it will fall pat as I told you.
— *A Midsummer Night's Dream* 5.1.184

Part scholarship, part journalism, part ecological screed, this book may read like an over-cooked batch of critical perspectives, a mashup of eco-criticism and close reading. Like other current investigations into the ecological significance of early modern literature, my account of *King Lear* draws on different and sometimes contrasting interpretive methods — cognitive science, evolutionary psychology, literary historicism, and what is called the new materialism. Moreover, I reflect on the broad global setting of eco-materialism's themes of catastrophe and enmeshed co-existence, using examples from Japan, New Mexico, Finland, India, all while jumping back to Shakespeare's early modern England. I also frame texts and genres in specific transcultural pairings: I ask that we think about Japanese tradition to understand European Renaissance pedagogy, and I make references to American pop culture — horror films and science fiction — to get at early modern drama's aesthetic effect.

No doubt the book wears this geographical and discursive motley because of the context of its making, being a product of an overseas sabbatical year in Tokyo. Reading Shakespeare's *King Lear* while sitting under three tiers of incessantly busy freeway overpasses in one of the world's most densely populated cities, in a sea of Roppongi neon and fifty-foot live-feed Sony ads, where Japan's techno-futurism sounds over the wave of urban commuters dressed in the weird nostalgia that defines Tokyo fashion — sleek faux-50s-American business suits or the cos-play of Lolita teeny bop dyed hair — all while, a few miles to the north, the Fukushima nuclear power plant silently leaks radiation into the Pacific. Lotus eaters lost in the funhouse? Or survivors clinging to outmoded rituals in the face of madness? In this context, reading for the kernel of Shakespeare's philosophy of the human in his great tragedy can feel a bit unsettling, like that of a posthuman Rorschach test. (Or a bad acid trip flashback of a Rorschach test.) No excuse, I suppose, but in this setting the interpretation of cosmic decay and ecological catastrophe in Shakespeare's great tragedy does not feel necessarily forced. Only suspiciously apparent.

If my book seems to switch gears, then, or leave off in one direction and go in another, it is not just because it is the product of seemingly incoherent modes of intellectual inquiry. It is primarily because it comes out of the frenetic urban existence whose current prospects seem fraught with the euphoria of abundance and the specter of peril. When considering how these problems are identified and talked about differently in different academic circles, it is really difficult to imagine that one book can bring these discourses and their audiences together to work on the literary text coherently. Twisting a rope of sand, as the adage goes. Just at the level of audience, those interested in ecology might not be interested in the history of Renaissance literacy. And those interested in the scholarship on Shakespeare's *King Lear* might not be interested in accounts of tsunami stones or radioactive waste sites. But they should be. I think it is worth taking the risk of sounding incoherent or boorish or alarmist in the face of ecological catastrophe. It is not risking all that much when considering the stakes. I feel strongly that the new trend in early modern literature to study seriously the sciences, especially ecological sciences, and the new philosophical turn to eco-materialism, or scientific realism as it is sometimes called, is absolutely necessary and exceedingly important. It is not just because we are likely to produce new accounts of old texts — posthuman studies has been doing this for years now — but because the proverbial clock is ticking. What Hamlet said about readiness? Well, it's happening. The sparrow has already fallen.

Shakespeare's *King Lear* does not, however, directly explore the first world urban experience. Rather, it gets at the deeper philosophical question of how we define human need in the context of a world where everything has been made to cater to the whims of a dying social system. The play offers a tantalizing account of humans at odds with the limits of their built environment. This is what I will call the posthuman parable of the narrative: during the course of the play the king learns that true need — defined in terms of love, charity, emotional recognition — is not something that can be ordered up like a plate of hasenpfeffer. Lear has this insight after struggling to resume his earlier status as sovereign subject, only to discover that at each turn he is becoming indistinguishable from those who live in the impoverished world outside his court. Lear learns that we need something that is in *excess* or outside of rational, calculable knowledge of our physical needs (here defined as food, housing, water). The tragedy not only stages the knotty issues of freeing ourselves from the logic of *homo economicus* — theories of production and consumption that are implicated in the enlightenment project of progress — but also in the way it imagines humans enmeshed as objects of a decaying world. In this way *King Lear* enacts the posthuman, reproducing in emblematic terms the critical impasse that evolves when trying to think beyond older categories that place human want and need in the context of class and status. Moreover, it urges us to think through the crucial gap in current critical thinking between old and new materialism, where the latter wants to eschew "constructionist" theories as somehow responsible for promoting the human experience as the only touchstone to value existence on our planet. This road of bracketing any and all old materialist theories is paved with good intentions, I'm sure. Lost in the fray of the debates between speculative realists and cultural materialists, however, is the acknowledgment that from the outset anti-humanism as a critical project always meant to de-center bourgeois (male) subjectivity as universal. The way the old materialism asserts its value to eco-criticism is to remind practitioners of the new object-oriented criticism that the Anthropocene just didn't happen, but evolved like a slow slouching beast over a long process of economic human activity best chronicled by materialist histories of urbanization and socialization. If eco-materialists work to rethink life in this wholly human-made geological era, it is best to think not of jettisoning the old theories that chart this process, but recycling its theories of causality and privileged terms of exchange and alienation.

Years ago, when I started teaching *King Lear,* I found it difficult to understand why the characters near the end of the play zone out and use a very different register to sound their words — zombie talk, I told my students — as if they were speaking to themselves out loud. They are not speaking through soliloquy *per se.* It is more like they are in shock. This makes sense, considering their circumstances. At first glance, it appears as if these characters — Lear, Edgar, Kent, and Gloucester — are reminding themselves of some adage about life's cruelty, seeking wisdom through the mode of speaking in the proverb. This comes to a head in the final words in the play, where Edgar leaves the audience hanging with the odd sing-songy lines, "Speak what we feel, not what we ought to say. / The oldest have borne most; we that are young / Shall never see so much, nor live so long." Blogs and online student crib-note pages respond to these lines succinctly: "what's up with the ending of *King Lear?*" The scholarly response echoes this frustration in a different key, perhaps, by avoiding the basic question of meaning to ponder the difference between the quarto and folio.[1] I will argue in this book that Shakespeare is staging this practice of speaking proverbs — collecting and using adages — and showing us its therapeutic value as a form of collective speech in times of

---

1   Put simply, the 1608 printed quarto version features Albany saying these lines, while the 1623 folio assigns them to Edgar. It makes sense, to me, to see Hemings and Condell, the actors who may have played these characters, switching this to the "younger" of the two, given the content of the line. I will state here that all my references to *King Lear* are to the Oxford conflated text as it appears in *The Norton Shakespeare,* 2nd edn. (London: Norton, 2008).

stress. This relates to the posthuman debate in two ways. First, in the way it figures the human subject as a kind of receptacle or automaton who repeats a program written long ago in the "dark backward and abysm of time."[2] Second, in the way these adages are written to offer counsel and succor for future strife. I think that Shakespeare was thinking of this literacy when writing *King Lear*. It is clear he was thinking about it when writing some of his other tragedies, particularly *Hamlet*.

One scene in *Hamlet* comes to mind. It's a scene much noted by scholars working on memory studies. Polonius is saying goodbye to his son Laertes, who is leaving for Paris, and he gives him some parting wisdom in the form of what he calls "precepts." Here, put these to memory. "Character" them, he says. And thus begins a litany of stock maxims: "Be thou familiar, but by no means vulgar" (1.3.81). *Et cetera*. In the Renaissance, this form of learning choice phrases from one's study, and collecting them in one's commonplace book, was a central part of education. It is a tradition that defined the very routine of reading and translating the past. Shakespeare's *Hamlet* foregrounds this literacy in different ways: Hamlet seems to be unlike Laertes in that his intellect appears entirely free from rote memory (the scene where he encounters his father's ghost is famous for Hamlet's use of the metaphor because he says he will tear all the pages out of his commonplace book in order to start fresh and just remember his father's murder). Later in the play, in the scene with Osric — the horribly awkward hanger-on of Claudius's court — Hamlet seems to make fun of people who have memorized words to help them through the strained conversations at court. One interesting metaphor is used by Hamlet to imagine the nature of this rote memory and its role in shaping one's intellect. It is used to describe Osric, so it's meant as a slur. Hamlet says:

> He did comply, sir, with his dug before he sucked it. Thus
> has he — and many more of the same bevy that I know the

2   The line is Prospero's from *The Tempest*, 1.2.50.

> drossy age dotes on — only got the tune of the time and
> outward habit of encounter, a kind of yeasty collection,
> which carries them through and through the most fond and
> winnowed opinions; and do but blow them to their trial, the
> bubbles are out. (5.2.140–46)

The words memorized from many primers and handbooks used by courtiers and clerks for their "winnowed opinions" are pictured here as a kind of frothy mix, a "yeasty collection." It is tantalizing to think of this idea of yeast — an ecological metaphor having to do with early modern cooking and diet — as a contradictory image (I think it's about beer and not sourdough). As suggested in the figurative language, this form of reading and memorizing adages is formative, it "writes the individual subject," as we would say, in that the teachers of Latin and Greek during the time had no illusions about giving students freedom to explore and find themselves in free writing or expressive modes of communication, as we believe today. Students were asked to memorize everything. As my own Latin instructor used to say at the beginning of class, parodying the stodgy teacher from the television show *The Paper Chase,* "we learn Latin the old fashioned way, we memorize it." But this image of yeast suggests that Shakespeare saw something potentially self-generating about the rote practice of memorizing maxims and integrating them into our own conversation, a fixed set of words that grows and grows into something more than the sum of its parts. It's supposed to be a negative image. Light. Frothy. Insubstantial. "Blow them to their trials, the bubbles are out."

Not so fast. In the sixteenth century the housewife would make the day's beer by using yesterday's yeast. It was never, in a sense, "out." Yeast keeps reproducing. Yeast cells reproduce through binary fission, which means that their DNA simply reproduces exact copies of itself — machine like — *ad infinitum.* And quickly. Millions of cells a day. Buried in this metaphor of the yeasty collection is Shakespeare's divided response to his own education: Hamlet's quick wit and imagination, how his mind doesn't seem to be held down by any single train of thought, rather it is made possible by a yeasty collection of adages, maxims, rhetorical gestures that are ingested in the imagination and then magically, endlessly, produce further rumination. Though Hamlet wants to put down Osric for being a twit with a fake personality, he nonetheless touches on the one aspect of humanist education that characterized its machine-like ability to churn out generations of "yeasty" wits, and playwrights whose work notably regenerated the writing of the past into some of the most dazzling literature in the English language.

King Lear is also reflecting on its educational origins, but in an entirely different key. If Hamlet's free-ranging mode of address can be described as an ebullient assessment of humanist training, *King Lear*'s staging of humanist learning is dour. The use of rhetoric in the play does not offer an image of regenerative nature. If anything, the picture of nature we get in *King Lear* is notoriously corrupted, "ruined," innately putrescent. And the two forms of "talking in script" are either coming from people who are masking their intentions and trying to deceive others, or from people who are going through their internal playbooks looking for a way to explain their bleak circumstances. I believe *King Lear* is one of the greatest experiments in humanist literacy, a wildly self-reflexive and profoundly probing work of art aimed at dislocating the power of state and church. When the dust settles, the characters are so alienated from their earlier faith as to be left only with the outer shell of its rituals, a forced pharisaical skepticism, where rote language is offered as a solution to the narrative's vision of social dissolution. If there is any hope offered in the view of rote memory in this play, it is not through an ecologically-minded figure of regeneration but in the image of characters using a form of affected speech whose familiar patterns and cadences offer a modicum of relief from the stress of their environment.

In Chapter One, "Listening to the Past; Or, How to Speak to the Future?" I frame the idea of rhetorical training and the use of adages in the context of our environmental crisis. I do this by showing how the collection of adages can be read as cautionary markers to be heeded by future readers. This is how Erasmus meant his book of adages to serve his future readers. I then shift gears and turn to Shakespeare's general use of the adage. I show how his work offers two types of proverbs: embedded and citational. The former is closer to the textbook example of a writer using the deeper truth of the common saw in the background of a particular line or image. The latter is more a self-conscious use of the proverb, citing or "quoting" the lines, in the course of one's own language. In Chapter Two, "*Lear* and the Proverbial Reflex," I offer my own reading of proverbs in *Lear*. In the beginning of the play, characters use proverbs like Osric. They are advancing an agenda, proffering wisdom but really masking an inward intent. When the play follows Lear to the heath, the use of proverbs changes and we are presented with scenes where ecological stress and nature's decay are forcing characters to retreat to the adage to reflect on their well-being. In Chapter Three, "Accessorizing *King Lear* in the Anthropocene," I move to reading the play as a parable about prodigality, where the shift to proverbial language as warning and caution is in keeping with the play's move from the ostentatious court to the denuded heath. It is in this chapter where I bring together the two theoretical strains of my book on memory studies and posthuman theory, looking at the subtext of aristocratic eating habits and the enmeshed ecology these habits imply in the play's thinking about Lear's self-examination. In the Coda, "*Lear*'s Receding World," I consider the theoretical implications of recuperating unconscious forms of human behavior as liberatory. I end with a few notes about the challenge of reading early modern literary texts as reflections on an imperiled ecology and why we cannot give in to the fatalism suggested by the overwhelming apocalyptic evidence. I argue that the trend to see from the vantage point of the object — the decentering of the human in the idea of a flat ontology — can potentially give in to this fatalism.

My argument about *Lear* is made in the full light of the day, as it were, with the humility that comes from knowing much of the scholarship on Shakespeare's indebtedness to rhetorical traditions has been done (and redone) years ago. In fact, one of the pestering fears with any approach to his work is the idea that there is nothing new to say. At least it seems so. His work has been revered and studied for so long, scholarship on his work is so robust and varied, that it feels like there is really nothing new that can be said. It's a pestering little truth Shakespeareans rarely talk about. Sure, we may put on a different face when speaking with colleagues in other fields. But when alone, when talking about "work" as readers, students, teachers, and scholars of Shakespeare, what we say is something entirely different. It's a fact of life for Shakespeareans best pondered in our own proverbs about "no stone left unturned," or "no meat left on the bone." (One colleague described it to me as "Shakespeare's been bled.") It drives some of us to antic despair, to drink, to concordances, to write epic footnotes that read like echoes in the Folger Shakespeare Library's vaulted rooms. We talk of the weird, *unheimliche* nature of Shakespeare scholarship, where it seems each of the great interpretations of his writing read sometimes, oddly, like re-packaged older arguments in new forms.

So this is to say I am fully aware I am making my own claims in a lively context and rich archive of historical scholarship on Shakespeare and *King Lear*. Many of the examples of proverbs I cover in the first chapter have been made by others (I make these references clear in my notes). Moreover, opposed to this ennui that comes from the thought there is nothing left to say, there are many inspiring arguments about the posthuman in Shakespeare studies today. It is no surprise that it is already a finely mapped territory whose perspectives and critical vocabulary offer new insights into humans as machines, human consciousness as a constructed, "written" program, or looking at the human–animal divide as an illusion meant to shore up priorities and exceptions to our species. I try to signal the overlapping of my insights with those made in posthuman Shakespeare studies clear as I go, especially in my coda. Finally, Shakespeare's indebtedness to mnemonic literacy is well established through history of the book and memory studies. I want to bring these conversations together to show how the Renaissance idea of rote literacy parallels ideas today about the posthuman body immersed in its environment. Rather than show how the text promotes the illusion of a human exceptionalism, a critical reading strategy offered by many eco-material readings ensconced in a no less modernist mode of interpreting texts as unmasking their ideologies, I argue that *King Lear* stages a form of enmeshed being where humans enact an autonomic conditioned response, reliving the internalized transhistorical collective speech of the adage.

Another caveat that is worth mentioning here is that the study of proverbs, *paramiology,* is its own intellectual tradition within different disciplinary investments, in psychology, linguistics, and folk studies.[3] It is not to be discounted because of the way it can provide what could be called a Bloomian middlebrow or amateur intellectual engagement with literature and the arts. A cursory glance at the Internet will provide many examples of the age-old Renaissance tradition of commonplacing: exhibiting sage advice and counsel through snippets of passages culled from the great authors. But the analysis of proverbs in cognitive sciences and folk traditions is vibrant. I run the risk of taking these approaches for granted if I assume they are working, like the others, free from an historical awareness of the roots of this pedagogy in medieval and Renaissance scholasticism. I try to capitalize on the cognitive science, as I do with the other scientific discourses that define posthuman and eco-materialism today, in my exploration of the mental processes involved when speaking through proverbs. The use of proverbs to garner support for one's political perspective, masking the universal wisdom of one's retrograde politics, is one of the long traditions that haunt *paramiology*. Using common saws to naturalize one's racial stereotypes, for example, is part of the ugly side of any genealogy of a rhetorical strategy. I hope it is clear enough that my flirting with the collective wisdom offered in the adage is made eyes wide open, as they say, to this history of modern invoca-

---

3   See Robert P. Honeck's *A Proverb in Mind: The Cognitive Science of Proverbial Wit and Wisdom* (London: Lawrence Erlbaum, 1997) for a good overview of the approaches.

tions of folk cultures to help shape the commons and its future.[4] If my own romantic conjuring of this received wisdom comes through in my writing, I imagine that I am being swayed by Erasmus's enthusiasm for his own archeological project.

Introductions to academic books can feel sometimes like the brave undoing of their creative acts, like that of Bottom and his rustic crew in *A Midsummer Night's Dream*. In the ways they have to account for their design and intentions, the fearless bunch attempts to explain every gesture and convention to their upcoming production, cutting a hole in Snug's mask to tell the ladies it's not a real lion. "You shall see, it will fall pat as I told you."

I am talking about the book. Not the sparrow.

---

4   See Wolfgang Mieder's *The Politics of Proverbs: From Traditional Wisdom to Proverbial Stereotypes* (Madison: University of Wisconsin Press, 1997).

CHAPTER ONE

Listening to the Past;
Or, How to Speak to the Future?

Is this the promised end?
— *King Lear* 5.3.263

…the world, which seems
To lie before us like a land of dreams,
So various, so beautiful, so new,
Hath really neither joy, nor love, nor light,
Nor certitude, nor peace, nor help for pain;
And we are here as on a darkling plain
Swept with confused alarms of struggle and flight ….
— Matthew Arnold, "Dover Beach"

Imagining our Material Contexts

As I write this, sitting in my office in my apartment in Minato-ku, Tokyo, there is, just two hundred kilometers from me, what eco-materialist critics call an assemblage of objects conspiring to tether me and my immediate world to its chain of causation.[1] Every day eighty thousand gallons of radioactive water leaks into the Pacific Ocean from the Fukushima Daiichi Nuclear Power Plant. This is about a gallon a minute. If you are reading these words at the average rate of 250 per minute, let's say, you will start and finish this paragraph as another couple gallons of

---

1   Jane Bennett, *Vibrant Matter: A Political Ecology of Things* (Durham: Duke University Press, 2010), 20–40.

contamination drains into Ishinomaki Bay and into the eastern Pacific basin. At the time of this writing, this free flow of contamination is unabated and will effectively continue, its power to mutate cumulatively growing. Tracing this dissemination of radioactivity is a lesson in what new materialists call the dispersal of agency across the "surface" of a slow moving but no less immanent event. The isotopes cesium 134 and 137 are water-soluble (cesium 137, one of the most deadly products of fission, has a half-life of thirty years). These radiated particles are dissolving in seawater and dispersing throughout the different layers of the ocean, at different rates depending on wind, currents, weather patterns, into plants, single cell organisms, causing a bioaccumulation of radioactive compounds in those animals at the top, "up" the ladder of the food chain.[2] Though scientists do not see humans beings immediately threatened by the fallout, it is easy to imagine the exponential spike of long term bio-magnification within this chain, especially given the main source of protein for islanders of Honshu, Tokyo's Tsukiji Fish Market, which sells 2,000 tons of seafood on average each day.

You have every right to think it is absurd to read an academic book in literary studies purporting to offer yet another "*Lear* in Our Times," and to be abruptly asked to consider the depressing

---

2   One fear is that marine phytoplankton in the surface waters of the sea basin, responsible for photosynthesizing oxygen, will be killed off. David Pacchioli, "How Is Fukushima's Fallout Affecting Marine Life?" *Oceanus Magazine,* May 2, 2013, http://www.whoi.edu/oceanus/feature/how-is-fukushimas-fallout-affecting-marine-life. An article by Ken O. Buesseler et al. is typical of the way some are downplaying the immediate threat of cesium 137 (with a half-life of 30 years) to humans. "Fukushima-derived Radionuclides in the Ocean and Biota off Japan," *Proceedings of the National Academy of Sciences* 109.16 (2012): 5984–88: DOI: 10.1073/pnas.1120794109, http://www.pnas.org/content/109/16/5984. But an article by Atsuki Hiyama et al. is representative of how others see significant effects of genetic mutation in the near future. The "indicator species" — the grass blue butterfly — portends other genetic mutations in the food chain. "The Fukushima Nuclear Accident and the Pale Grass Blue Butterfly: Evaluating Biological Effects of Long-term Low-dose Exposures," BMC *Evolutionary Biology* 13.168 (August 12, 2013): DOI: 10.1186/1471–2148–13–168, http://www.biomedcentral.com/1471–2148/13/168.

image of the Fukushima Daiichi facility poisoning our Pacific rim ecosystem. Judging the vast scale of the potential future damage, the repercussions to generations of life on the planet in the long term, my gesture here must appear sensational, if not histrionic. However, if we take seriously the challenge of the new eco-materialism to imagine ourselves impacted by the object world around us, it is easy to reverse the terms of the question and ask, why are we considering another perspective on *Lear* at all when such a thing is happening? Another way to put this might be to force the question: how can we imagine doing the work of literary studies and *not* consider such an eco-material context? How could we plod on without appearing like we are repressing some terrifying truth that figures like the old medieval theme of mortality, a new existential horizon whose bounds can promise no safe passage? At the very least, it seems an important question to ask — perhaps *the* question — as another two gallons of water tainted with deadly radioactive isotopes lap into the turbid brine.

This is not to mention the countless millions of gallons that have been dumped since the March 2011 earthquake and tsunami occurred. How do we ponder such a bleak image? Imagining a post-apocalyptic future is one of the things Shakespeare's *King Lear* is about. At least, this is where it leaves us in the end. On the beach, among the bodies, with no real plan to move forward, but with a few austere adages about what we've learned from our mistakes. But this simple awareness of the ecological challenges of our day does not seem enough in the face of the rising tide. For all of its sophisticated philosophical evacuations of the old epistemic critical categories, perhaps the greatest challenge of the "new" materialism is that it demands that we rethink causality, ideas of agency, and reexamine the present in the context of a doubtful posthuman future. Imagining the end is where eco-material posthuman theory begins. I want to eventually get to the second-order philosophical unraveling implied in the title of my book, but I want to start here, at the end, on the beach, as it were, to frame one important textual feature of Shakespeare's great tragedy with our current ecological present. Assemblages and complicated causality work both ways. They can effect ripples in our environments as well as our interpretative systems. We start with unpacking a hermeneutic riddle in Shakespeare's play: why do characters speak in proverbs? And, like a juggler on the beach tossing washed up items in the air, we soon find ourselves juggling it all, early modern rhetorical devices, Renaissance educational practices, inheritance of Lucian stoicism, clashing ideologies evinced in the text, not to mention readerly techniques and dispositions — close reading, affective theories, modernist aesthetic philosophy, disappearing philosophical categories replaced with new. The soapy episteme is mixed at our ankles, and waves touching our thoughts on early modern theater do not pose an immediate threat, but we have time to sort it out, for the time being.

The posthuman will be foregrounded in my reading of Shakespeare as the unformed, "emergent" discourse allowed to speak in our present context. Hugh Grady has defined in the corpus of his critical works this approach as *presentist* historicism, a rigorous contextualizing where "the past takes on new contours and qualities for us as our thinking shifts in the present."[3] "Our knowledge of works of the past," he continues, "is conditioned by and dependent upon the culture, language, and ideologies of the present, and this means that historicism itself necessarily produces an implicit allegory of the present in its configuration of the past."[4] Indebted to the Frankfurt School and especially to Adorno's dialectical method, Grady is careful to acknowledge that the moment of identification in the critical act is one based on seeing oneself in the otherness of the past: "part of this work of reinterpretation involved coming to understand how and why themes of late modernity might have been produced in the discourses of early modernity in the forms close enough to our own to seem cognate to us."[5] I think it is fitting to

3   Hugh Grady, *Shakespeare, Machiavelli, and Montaigne: Power and Subjectivity from Richard II to Hamlet* (Oxford: Oxford University Press, 2002), 2.
4   Ibid.
5   Ibid.

frame an analysis of William Shakespeare's most nihilistic narrative about cosmic decay by foregrounding the problem of our
own uncertain future. Shakespeare's *King Lear* desacralizes the
old-world ideals that informed Jacobean culture. The tragedy
depicts wide-scale destruction of war and social cataclysm as
a backdrop to the King's story of domestic rule and his ensu-
ing madness. "In the epilogues to the Histories and Tragedies,"
Jan Kott reminds us, "the new monarch invites those present to
his coronation. In *King Lear* there will be no coronation. There
is no one whom Edgar can invite to it. Everybody has died or
been murdered....Those who have survived — Edgar, Albany,
and Kent — are, as Lear has been, 'just ruin'd pieces of nature.'"[6]

Thinking about the scientific problem of surviving in
the Anthropocene, and especially the disposal of nuclear
waste — whose radioactivity remains dangerous for hundreds of
thousands of years — helps us imagine the terror about physical
dissolution evinced in *Lear*. In this tragedy, Shakespeare articulates a morbid fixation with nature's decay, and the radical indifference that time and nature have to human life. When compared to his other tragedies, *King Lear* seems to offer no future,
no way to think beyond its ending. On Shakespeare's Dover
Beach, there remains no surviving character to show the world
how to rebuild from the carnage. Scholars have tried to explain
the tragedy's aesthetic effect as a kind of exorcism or evacuation
of medieval feudal customs, an interrogation of the moral system so devastating that it leaves nothing in its wake to imagine
a new one.[7] Kott, whose brave ear confronted the nihilism of the

6   Jan Kott, *Shakespeare Our Contemporary* (London: Methuen, 1965), 120–21.
7   William Elton's description of the "The Problem" (Chapter One) in his *King
    Lear and the Gods* (Chicago: Huntington Library, 1966) summarizes this
    historically rich scholarly debate, where, in his mind anyway, Shakespeare's
    depiction of pagan animism presents serious "obstacles" to the Christian
    reading. In my opinion, Maynard Mack's *King Lear in Our Time* (Berkeley:
    University of California Press, 1972) is the well source of many contempo-
    rary readings of *King Lear*'s skepticism. Also see Graham Bradshaw's idea of
    "perspectivism" in his *Shakespeare's Scepticism* (New York: St. Martin Press,
    1987), and Millicent Bell's idea of "skeptical disillusion" in *Shakespeare's
    Tragic Skepticism* (New Haven: Yale University Press, 2002). The idea that

play and who famously read *King Lear* through Samuel Beckett's avant-garde theater, described modern productions approaching the "absurd mechanism" of the play's destruction free from salvation. "Various kinds of impersonal and hostile mechanisms have taken the place of God, Nature and History, found in the old tragedy. The notion of an absurd mechanism," he continues, "is not transcendental any more in relation to man, or at any rate to mankind. It is a trap set by man himself into which he has fallen."[8] I think there is a way to read Shakespeare's tragedy that recognizes and reworks this posthuman kernel of its absurd mechanism. When Matthew Arnold wrote "Dover Beach," I have to imagine that the poem's bleak image of the world was meant to respond to Shakespeare's last scene on Dover Beach in *King Lear*. Arnold is using the play, at least tangentially, to think about the nihilism of his own time; the poem's question-

---

Shakespeare's "aesthetic distancing" of even his own disillusion — that his own doubt is framed with poetic ambivalence — teases at some of this scholarship. John Cox's idea of "skeptical faith" in *Seeming Knowledge: Shakespeare and Skeptical Faith* (Waco: Baylor University Press, 2007) attempts to square this circle by framing the question of Shakespeare's doubt within a religious discourse, a strong trend in the last twenty years to read Shakespeare as Catholic and all his mysteries as recusancy. Much of the current historicist readings attempt to frame Shakespeare's skepticism in classical antecedents or through his reading of Montaigne, or trace this ambivalence through sixteenth-century contradictions in political and economic forces: Stephen Greenblatt's "Shakespeare and the Exorcists," in *Shakespearean Negotiations: The Circulation of Social Energy in Renaissance England* (Berkeley: University of California Press, 1988), discusses Shakespeare's distancing gestures in the context of Reformation critiques of Catholic ritual, while Jonathan Dollimore's *Radical Tragedy: Religion, Ideology and Power in the Drama of Shakespeare and his Contemporaries* (Chicago: University of Chicago Press, 1984) and Richard Halpern's *The Poetics of Primitive Accumulation: English Renaissance Culture and the Genealogy of Capital* (Cornell, NY: Cornell University Press, 1991) place the idea of decentered subjectivity in the neo-Marxist contexts of Althusserian critiques of power and "primitive accumulation" respectively. Grady's *Shakespeare, Machiavelli, and Montaigne* argues forcefully that there is a trajectory from political critique to doubt. For current framing of this topic, see the special Open Review "Shakespeare and Skepticism" in *Shakespeare Quarterly*, ed. Joseph Loewenstein, http://shakespearequarterly.folger.edu/openreview/?page_id=4.

8   Kott, *Shakespeare Our Contemporary*, 105.

ing of faith, its existential doubt, and finally its secular humanism, are nevertheless released through the allusion. As its own
actant, the reference to *Lear* lingers in the margins of the poem,
activating a series of recognitions, mental cognates. One reads
the poem and thinks of Kent walking off the stage to a dubious
end. And when returning to *King Lear,* one thinks of Arnold's
"confused alarms of struggle and flight." Arnold's "solution," if
we can call it this, to the problem posed by nature's indifference is to see genuine community, the idea of being "true" to one
another as an effort to solidify sustaining social bonds (friendship? love?) in age where the older paradigms seem mute and
no longer speak to us. It's a solution that elegantly frames *King
Lear's* radical skepticism. Another way to see Arnold's reading,
however, is to consider how its own solution reproduces the
crude mechanical logic of the world it opposes, the panicked
moment of discovery — "if no faith, then I will accept a secular
love" — that admits its attitude toward communalism is a last
resort. This is a crude rendering, but it gets to the logic of much
literary criticism of Shakespeare's tragedy, which similarly re-
coils at the profound skepticism of the play, and then reaches
out to find something to explain this lack of redemption.[9] Star-
ing at the stark reality presented in the play, critics wince and
then attempt to see some hope offered in its silences.

I want to believe that Shakespeare's play helps us identify the
posthuman in our time, especially in the way it grapples with
this idea of imagining the future. I want to explore this idea of
speaking to the future a bit more before returning to the play
itself. Take some time on the beach, with the bodies and the

9 I am indebted to John Cox's summary in *Seeming Knowledge* of the critical
debate about suffering in *Lear,* from Samuel Johnson, Nahum Tate, up to
Jan Kott, William Elton, and Maynard Mack. Maynard Mack comments that
Tate's revision is not wrong or willfully corrupting of the original. Rather,
Tate discovers the "romantic core" of the plot by allowing Cordelia and Lear
to live. Oddly, Mack doesn't mention *King Leir* as the Renaissance equivalent
to Tate's version, which is to say, the literary antecedents of *King Lear* that are
also romantic. Another way to put this might be that Shakespeare's play sees
the skeptical posthuman core in a story that is romantic for everyone else.

remains of social cataclysm, to think about the idea of reading literature to prepare, to *fit* ourselves. Literature as equipment, in Burke's famous formula, but also *equipping*. Literature as *equipping* for the future (I will speak more about Burke below). The posthuman kernel is here, on the beach. It is fitting to start, then, with one of the great critical paradoxes of the play offered by Edgar at the end (or Albany in *Q1*), when he tries to makes sense of Lear's death by signaling its meaning in a trite adage. Scholars tend to search for an aesthetic distance in the play's final rationalization of violence.[10] Some claim that the idea of alienation-effect institutionalized by Bertolt Brecht's modernism is indebted to Shakespeare's realism. As I will explore later, these moments of proverbial reflection seem "wrapped" in this critical overlay, as moments of alienation and thus critique, but as I will argue this is not the only way we have to read these passages. Reflecting on Lear's earlier transgression, Edgar's famous final lines provide for us nonetheless a way to reflect on one of the play's nostalgic strains. His words, "speak what we feel, not what we ought to say," carve a cautionary path forward, a way to parse the providential lesson of the play, what we might identify as the stoic lesson of Lear's precipitous fall. To move on, to keep living, remember to "speak what we feel." But is this really all that we are left with at the end? If we remember, we can avoid past mistakes and move on? Edgar is taking us back to the beginning, looking for that point in the past that triggered the tragic unfolding: Lear's question, "Which of you ... doth love us most?" (1.1.49). His adage also serves as a signpost to the notion of *desis,* tragedy's depiction of the protagonist's life caught in the web of past actions. Aren't we merely back where we started? Isn't a scripted answer to Lear's question... unethical?

Set this down. "Speak what we feel. Not what we ought to say." Remember it, and then, when asked, perform the prescript

---

10 One notorious "read" of the jarring simplicity of the ending, which I want to examine in more detail below, is Jonathan Dollimore's theory of the "refusal of closure" in *Radical Tragedy.* To me, Dollimore's reading of *King Lear* is formative. I speak more of this in the chapters below.

out of habit. Performing language out of habit would be recognizable to early modern teachers and scholars, trained as they were in the rote habits of memory and translation. But wait. If we write this down to memorize it, is it really what we feel when we say it? Isn't this the "glib and oily art" of artificial speech that got us into the trouble in the first place? This is Shakespeare's version of the philosophical liar's paradox — "this sentence is false" — but in this instance it is hard not to feel like a crude joke is being played on us as we try to parse through the semantic possibilities. If we remember to speak what we feel, the form of remembering to do this undermines the authenticity of the act of responding free from a rehearsed, mediated form. Like Arnold's attempt at finding hope in the face of the indifferent ebb, here we have a mechanical reaction to write lessons in the sand, find some solace in the wake of destruction. What interests me is the aphoristic quality of Edgar's advice, how the sharp proverbial form shapes the expression. If Edgar is meant to be a character of hope, say, like Fortinbras from *Hamlet,* a symbol for the promise of a new society that returns to the themes of duty and justice, then this very moment in the play teases us with the lingering image of rebuilding on such a sandy foundation. Edgar has borne witness to too many of the betrayals and moments of self-destruction to arrive as *deus ex machina.* One could make an argument that his challenge to Edmund renews justice and simulates the cult of blood and honor lost in the play's anatomy of Machiavellian politics, if it weren't for the fact that the decision itself is tinged with the same theater and stagecraft used by Edmund. Where do we begin parsing this quizzical use of proverb?

Warning Signs: Tsunami Stones and Eternal Markers

What if we were to approach these lines as an earnest attempt at survival? Edgar leaves everyone with a warning: his proverb is meant to work as cautionary sign. But how are we meant to read it? Where do these seemingly memorized lines come from? And what is their affect? How are we meant to listen to them? How

Figure 2. Aneyoshi Tsunami Stone. "The homes on higher places will guarantee the comforts of the descendants, Remind the horror of the tsunamis, do not build homes below this point. We suffered tsunamis in 1896 and also in 1933, only two villagers ... survived [*sic*]." Photo courtesy of Hatsuki Nishio. Photo taken June 14, 2013.

are we to interpret the seemingly endless uses of adages and proverbial speech in the rest of the play? Taking Edgar's lines as a microcosm, it is as if trauma induces Renaissance humanism to retreat into itself, to return to rote habit, but we are left realizing that, taking the play as a whole, this is perhaps both the cause and solution to the crisis. Edgar imagines speaking to the future: his first thought is to think of a way to avoid the tragedy again. I want to explore more of the history of proverbs and their value to Renaissance humanism. But first I want to return to the example of Japan and radiation to frame the idea of speaking to a deaf future in the context of our possible radioactive reckoning. I want to raise the stakes a bit through considering more our posthuman crisis. Are we learning our lesson? How do we think of speaking to the future? More tangents. A few more gallons.

To get at "it" — the cause or "object" responsible for the Fukushima meltdown in this case — means to unravel parts of the assemblage, the different *actants* responsible for the nuclear plant's destruction, which can read like tracing the hero's past actions in a tragedy. What was the original act that led to this moment? The seawater was responsible for the power outage. The power outage led to the pump's failure in the core. Was the earthquake responsible for the meltdown, then? Maybe the building of the plant to begin with? The ineffectual seawall? What about the tsunami itself? But what caused that? The earthquake? These quakes occur from of the force of the two tectonic plates — the Phillipine Sea Plate and the Eurasian Plate — crashing against each other. When the Eurasian Plate slips, it releases an awesome amount of kinetic energy, resulting in tremors. The quakes and tsunamis are part of the natural world in this region, like the tide and moon, part of the earth's eternal clock.

Because these earthquakes have gone on for centuries, people have learned to keep the collective memory of the natural danger alive through the use of special markers. Past generations in Japan knew of the dangers of tsunamis and built stone signposts meant to warn future generations of building houses and villages near the sea. Tsunami stones, as they are called, can be found up and down the northeastern shore of Honshu. They are made of flat tablets, some nine feet high, marking the dangerous limit of the tsunami's reach. "Do not build your homes below this point." Or: "High dwellings ensure the peace and happiness of our descendants."[11] The magnitude of the Tōhoku quake that triggered the March 2011 tsunami was not the worst experienced in Japan. One of the controversies surrounding the Fukushima Daiichi meltdown is the way the Tokyo Electric Power Company (TEPCO) — who own and manage the plant — handled the report written by geologist Yukinobu Okamura, three years before the crisis. Based on studies of the sand deposits in Sendai, Okamura calculated how powerful earlier tsunamis had been, confirming the legend that, as stated in *The True History of Three Reigns of Japan* (901 CE), inland castles were destroyed by waves resulting from the great "Jogan" quake of 869 CE.[12] As reported in Mark Willacy's *Fukushima and the Inside Story of the Nuclear Meltdowns,* the nuclear plant was built with outdated safeguards. Fukushima Daiichi was built to withstand six-meter tsunamis that result from magnitude six quakes thought to occur every 100 to 150 years.[13] The monster Tōhoku quakes in Okamura's study were at least eight-plus magnitude and resulted in 16.5-meter waves. "We discovered that the intervals between the tsunamis are 500 to 800 years. That means that if no quake had hit since the Jogan tremor, then the probability of [another large earthquake] was high" (100). TEPCO decided against building the necessary protective wall that may have shielded the power plant from the brunt of the tsunami's first waves.

Tsunami stones mark the impending danger: they are meant to speak the language of tomorrow, to warn people in the future

11 Martin Fackler, "Tsunami Warnings Written in Stone," *The New York Times,* April 20, 2011, http://www.nytimes.com/2011/04/21/world/asia/21stones.html?pagewanted=all&_r=0.

12 *Nihon Sandai Jitsuroku* ["The True History of Three Reigns of Japan"]. National history of Japan written in 901 CE. For translation see: Sakamoto Taro, *The Six National Histories of Japan.* (UBC Press: Tokyo, 1991), 169–186.

13 Mark Willacy, *Fukushima and the Inside Story of the Nuclear Meltdowns* (Sydney: Macmillan Australia, 2013), 100–104.

Figure 3. Tsunami stone of Attari.
Photo courtesy of Hatsuki Nishio. Photo taken September 12, 2015.

that this too will happen to them (*fig.* 2[14]). But to do this, they have to exist unchanged, fixed. These markers are meant to speak across generations to keep the lived memory of the cataclysmic from fading. The problem with the tsunami stones is that they are so old as to be taken as part of the natural landscape. There seems a limit to people's interest, a kind of crude news cycle to human memory. Fumihiko Imamura, a professor of urban studies specializing in disaster planning at Tōhoku University in Sendai, explains: "It takes about three generations for people to forget. Those that experience the disaster themselves pass it to their children and their grandchildren, but then the memory

14 See Aska, "Aneyoshi tsunami warning stone tablet," *Megalithic Portal,* June 22, 2013, http://www.megalithic.co.uk/article.php?sid=34248.

fades."[15] Pictures of the tsunami markers taken today often reveal this neglect, as they appear like forgotten monuments left to their own slow erosion among the cedars (*fig.* 3).

Tsunami stones are designed to function as universal warning signs to speak across the great generational divides to ensure the survival of the community. But how to speak across this divide in a language that is recognizable to people of tomorrow? In a language that can be understood?

This is precisely the problem the U.S. Environmental Protection Agency faced — on a much grander scale — when it attempted to devise a timeless warning sign, officially termed a "Passive Institutional Control," to caution future generations of the environmental hazard of nuclear radiation at its Waste Isolation Pilot Plant storage facility in the Delaware Basin outside Carlsbad, New Mexico. When considering the hazards of nuclear energy, perhaps the Carlsbad case is closer to home for most of us. This site, the third deepest storage facility in the world, is licensed to store nuclear waste permanently for more than a hundred thousand years. In this instance, given the half-life of the radioisotopes, the question of communicating to future generations about the lingering hazard of radiation is infinitely magnified. How to build tsunami stones that speak to generations this far in the future? To conceive of this span of time, one has to employ a geological time scale. Not only do civilizations come and go, but entire species can appear and fade from earth's memory. Instead of having to speak across the divide of three generations, the EPA had to imagine a moment so far in the future relative to the history of our own that the dump site could be inhabited by people who speak and think differently. How to conceive of a language to warn people (can we call them people? What will they call themselves?) living past the end of human time? But how to insure that the vital record of the past isn't lost in the weeds?

---

15 "Ancient Stone Markers Warned of Tsunamis," CBS *News,* April 6, 2011, http://www.cbsnews.com/news/ancient-stone-markers-warned-of-tsunamis/.

The EPA put together a panel of expert linguists, anthropologists, and sociologists to devise warning signs, a set of signposts, markers, and architectural structures that might speak to all readers of the future. N. Katherine Hayles's momentous book *How We Became Posthuman: Virtual Bodies in Cybernetics, Literature and Informatics* traces the origins of the idea of the posthuman as it emerged from the cognitive science developed out of sponsored academic "think tanks" in the post-war moment of cybernetics and "informatics."[16] Hayles could have easily included in her narrative the EPA's "Permanent Markers Team" because its consideration was to imagine the posthuman in the most literal of terms.[17] The "team" (teams, more properly) was to focus intently on the deadly environmental legacy of human life, not from a skeptical vantage point fueled by contemporary political debate, but as a foregone conclusion. Their plan, called "Permanent Markers Implementation Plan," involves a ghoulish architectural scheme installing huge, grotesque, and menacing fences spread across the desert, with signs made out of imperishable stones. The plan for this macabre theme park (what else do we call it?) proposes using colossal forms to warn people away from the site: berms, giant jagged iron posts, a "landscape of thorns" meant to look like the remnants of a war zone (*fig. 6, p. 46*[18]), including tall murals with menacing images of death, an entire built landscape designed to evoke instant threat. What is the best way to warn of the dangers of nuclear waste but to

16 N. Katherine Hayles, *How We Became Posthuman: Virtual Bodies in Cybernetics, Literature and Informatics* (Chicago: University of Chicago Press, 1999), 50–83.

17 The "team" I refer to above consisted of three specific groups looking at "drilling intrusions" (Boston Team), "inadvertent intrusions" (Southwest Team), and "decomposed judgments … probability of intrusion" (Washington Team). See Stephen C. Hora et al., *Expert Judgment on Inadvertent Human Intrusion into the Waste Isolation Pilot Plant,* Sandia National Laboratories Report SAND90–3063 / UC-721, December 1991, http://large.stanford.edu/courses/2011/ph241/dunn2/docs/SAND90–3063.pdf.

18 From Dieter G. Ast et al., "Excerpts from *Expert Judgment on Markers to Deter Inadvertent Human Intrusion into the Waste Isolation Pilot Plant*" (1993) [*sic*], http://downlode.org/Etext/WIPP/.

Figure 4. Permanent Marker Warning Sign.

reproduce an image of a fallen world, a world that suffered from its use?

If not for the seriousness of the design — its use of actual measurements, discussion of the best rock surfaces for the proper impression, considerations of visual sightlines, etc. — the plan would read like the brainchild of a brilliant ironic artist, the weirdest of parodies of postmodern architecture to visualize something like Disney's version of a *memento mori.* In creating such foreboding structures and on such a scale, the permanent markers reproduce the post-apocalyptic environment they warn against, a besieged city frozen at the end of time. The EPA's plan can be read as a grisly mirror to the old folk villages of the twentieth-century nation states, where the frontier past and the nation's identity is celebrated in a frozen "slice of life" from an imagined social setting, a tightly-bound community surviving scarcity through its peculiar means of cultural innovation in architecture and technology. Except in this instance, the post-nuclear folk community is captured at its end, frozen in the moment of colossal demise, a human village caught in its final moments not of thatched roofs, fermented wines, domesticated animals, but of desolation and squander. The "sense" the visitor is supposed to have of walking through the warning site, as described by the plan, reads like an allegory of human myopia. "Walking through it, at ground level, the massive earthworks crowd in on you, dwarfing you, cutting off your sight to the horizon, a loss of connection to any sense of place."[19] Interestingly, the warning signs consciously use an image based on Edward Munch's *The Scream* to denote terror, insuring that Munch's legacy may perhaps survive all other human art (*fig. 4*[20]).

These signs will be posted on 25-foot high monuments surrounding the area, and at the center — directly above the site — will sit an "information center" (like an Epcot Pavilion of Death) made of granite, featuring explanations in six different "U.N. recognized languages on archival paper" warning people to stay away, along with star charts of what the North Star and Big Dipper will look like when it is finally safe to inhabit the area (*fig. 5*).[21]

Reading the language for the center devised by the team, one cannot help but think it represents the worst kind of group-think of committee work:

> This place is a message … and part of a system of messages … pay attention to it! Sending this message was important to us. We considered ourselves to be a powerful culture. This is not a place of honor … no highly esteemed deed is commemorated here … nothing is valued here. What is here

19 Ibid.
20 See "Permanent Markers Implementation Plan," August 19, 2004, 28, http://www.wipp.energy.gov/library/PermanentMarkersImplementationPlan.pd
21 "How Will Future Generations be Warned?" Summary of Permanent Markers Implementation Plan, http://www.wipp.energy.gov/fctshts/warned.pdf, 3, 38.

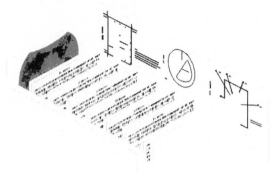

Figure 5. Information Center. "The conceptual design is an open structure, allowing observation of the contents of the building with natural light. It will consist of walls, floor, and panels made of granite."

is dangerous and repulsive to us. This message is a warning about danger.[22]

The EPA is hoping that this will scare away wary visitors. The "Permanent Markers Implementation Plan" is a bureaucratic document presenting the best way to communicate the legacy of nuclear radiation. The language of this plan is a teasingly morbid text that invites ironic readings. Nonetheless, it is difficult to shake the powerful image of these eternal markers. Tsunami stones for the posthuman, the permanent markers imagined here are made to confront time's decay in the New Mexico desert, to speak like a post-nuclear Ozymandias. One wonders if not, in the crudest of ironies, the constructed markers of the site

---

22   Ast et al., "Excerpts from *Expert Judgement on Markers.*"

will be readily recognizable as such, or if they will be indistinguishable from the fallen post-nuclear world around it.[23]

It is hard not to admire the idealism behind the plan of this gargantuan edifice. Anyone with young children, however, can tell you what the real effect of such warning "controls" will be. The elaborate markers and exotic granite kiosk could just as easily lure people to the site, especially those thinking the warnings are an elaborate ruse to chase looters away from the obvious treasures buried beneath. The real effect of these warning signs, in fact, may be to direct attention to the valuable manufactured metals used to compose the storage tanks under ground (steel, copper, and aluminum). The EPA's solution to warn future generations of the risk of buried radiation is nonetheless predicated on the premise that warning is better than just ignoring the possibility of a future breach to the storage site.

But is it? Consider Finland's radical decision to use no signs whatsoever — to "pull a Keyser Söze" — at its nuclear storage site, Onkalo repository at the Olkiluoto Nuclear Power Plant on the island of Olkiluoto. The Onkalo repository (the word *onkalo* means "hiding place") will be the biggest and deepest reposi-

---

23 Read Jeffrey Cohen's magisterial interpretation of the warning markers in his "Time out of Memory," in *Posthistorical Middle Ages*, ed. Elizabeth Scala and Sylvia Federico (London: Palgrave, 2009), 37–61. Cohen orients the reading of stone toward medieval studies and, more generally, a renewed interest in what he calls the "stillness of the past," a sense of the ahistorical that challenges a historicist investment in fixing time to a single vision. "Without a phenomenological awareness of the constant interaction of that which is time-bound and that which is transhistorical, even across inhuman temporal gaps, historicism as a critical practice can become an impoverished method of reading the past, reducing into stillness worlds that are animated and ever-changing" (56). In his latest book, *Stone: An Ecology of the Inhuman* (Minneapolis: University of Minnesota Press, 2015), Cohen elaborates on the idea of inhuman time and its application with the Yucca storage facility (111–13). His sympathetic reading of the warning signs as "the desire to send messages across inhuman spans through stone" is used to think about Stonehenge (113): "a project ... sent into that future to keep an ever-receding present alive through the accumulation of temporal heterogeneity" (114). *Stone* appeared in print after my manuscript had been submitted for review. Cohen is among the ecologically-minded scholars whose work I find inspiring.

Figure 6. Proposed image for "Landscape of Thorns."

tory at the time of its completion at the end of this century.[24] As documented in Danish director Michael Madsen's somber and creepy documentary, *Into Eternity: A Film for the Future,* the engineers of Onkalo's nuclear fuel repository were faced with the same problem of dealing with the radioactive waste.[25] Speaking about geological time, Peter Wikberg (Research Director, Nuclear Fuel and Waste Management, Sweden), explains in the documentary why the bedrock under Finland was the perfect choice for nuclear disposal: "At the surface, the earth's clock is very fast. While in the rock, it goes very slowly." Buried at such depths, the radiation has time to live through its half-life uninterrupted, to live on into a geological future that cannot be truly envisioned because we lack the mental cognates to "see" such distance realistically. Nonetheless, trying to picture what this moment might look like, the engineers turned to the past:

24 Julian Whitcrosse, "Finland's Brilliant Plan for Dealing with Nuclear Waste: Pulling a Keyser Söze," *io9,* May 13, 2012, http://io9.com/5909853/finlands-brilliant-plan-for-dealing-with-nuclear-waste-pulling-a-kaiser-soze.

25 Michael Madsen, dir., *Into Eternity: A Film for the Future* (Atmo Media Network, 2010).

MADSEN: Can we learn anything from the past that can help us communicate 100,000 years into the future?

MIKAEL JENSEN: (Analyst, Radiation Authority, Sweden): Usually when we look at these time scales we go back in time. And obviously, you see, we go back 100,000 years back in the past we come to our ancestors in Africa and we also cover as we go along our ancestors in Europe in the form of the "Neanderthal" ... "man." And you have to realize we have very little in common. How would you make parallel from people hunting mammoths with spears? It is difficult to explain with these people something about nuclear waste. We cannot assume that people or creatures of the future will understand very much.

MADSEN: But is it also clear that they may have different kinds of senses then we have?

JENSEN: Yes, senses, appearances, needs, and knowledge. Everything goes away. There is no one true statement that will then survive.[26]

Jensen's articulation of the problem, that "there is no one true statement that will then survive," sets the stage for their radical departure from the EPA's attempt at conceiving of nuclear warning signs. What if the sign lures rather than frightens? Intrigues rather than warns? Deep down under the planet's surface in the bedrock, the earth's clock is slow, and above, life is subject to the forces of wars, pestilence, climate changes, and ecological collapse. Nonetheless, the EPA remains convinced that their warning signs in Carlsbad will serve as nuclear tsunami stones to the future. It is an impressive idealism in the face of uncertainty.

I would argue that an equivalent to the eternal "cautionary marker" can certainly be found in the Renaissance context. The gesture of imagining the future by thinking of the past, the fascination with perdurable language bridging gaps in myth and culture: these were the obsessions of the Renaissance humanist. For the scholars of the sixteenth century, the earth's clock was frozen; people felt while reading the ancients that they were

26 Madsen, dir., *Into Eternity.*

the equivalents of Jensen's mammoth hunters living after the fall of the great civilizations of the past. Did they have what they needed to survive? What today's nuclear scientist calls "passive institutional controls," the early modern humanist might recognize as the proverb.

Renaissance Proverbs: Casting Stones

> There is … in these proverbs some native authentic power of truth. Otherwise how could it happen that we should frequently find the same thought spread abroad among a hundred peoples, transposed into a hundred languages, a thought which has not perished or grown old even with the passing of so many centuries, which pyramids themselves have not withstood?
> — Erasmus, *Adages*[27]

> A proverb … is a ruin which stands on the site of an old story and in which a moral twines about a happening like ivy around a wall.
> — Walter Benjamin[28]

Renaissance humanists had an answer to the question about how to speak across millennial divides. On its face, the question itself would seem silly, nearly unthinkable, to an early modern humanist trained to read history as a timeless window into the present. The awareness exhibited by Jensen's scientific analysis of human consciousness against the backdrop of geological time might appear exotic or foreign to early modern readers who so readily identified with the ancient authors. The idealism assumes a deeper correspondence between present and past, and one that places early modern thought at odds with modernity

---

27 Desiderius Erasmus, *The Adages of Erasmus,* ed. William Barker (Toronto: University of Toronto Press, 2001), 16.
28 Walter Benjamin, "The Storyteller: Reflections on the Works of Nikolai Leskov," in *Illuminations,* trans. Harry Zohn (New York: Schocken Books, 1969), 108.

and ideas of historical difference. Nonetheless, scholars in the sixteenth century were aware of time's erosive effects and had at their fingertips countless examples of civilizations that faded into memory, whose only proof of existence at all remained in the teasing chronologies of historians like Herodotus.[29] The adage was a root-stock practice of humanist education, as we will see, and it left a legacy hard to ignore, as readers today might walk through the early modern arts and letters and see the adage strewn about the various fields and, like the neglected tsunami stones, not notice them for the trees.

From the fifteenth century on, adages were used predominantly in exercise books to teach Latin and Greek translation. Collecting of the "adage" in one's commonplace or journal while reading was the principle reading strategy. "Thou shalt have always at hande a paper booke," Juan Luis Vives instructs in his *Ad sapientiam introductio* (1524), "wherein thou shalt wryte suche notable thynges as thou readest thy selfe, or hearest of other men worthi to be noted, be it other feate sentence or worde, meete for familiar speech, that thou mayste have in redynes, when tyme requyreth."[30] "As his studies grew and his attitude toward Latin matured," Rudolph Habenicht describes in his "The Proverb Tradition in Early Sixteenth-Century," "the pupil learned the proverb as a rhetorical figure of speech with which he might embellish his theme, or help an argument by the authority of

29 See Siep Stuurman's analysis of Herodotus's theme in the Histories of the "transience of greatness" which "precludes the lasting success of any imperial venture" in "Herodotus and Sima Qian: History and the Anthropological Turn in Ancient Greece and Han China," *Journal of World History* 19.1 (2008): 17 [1–40]. See also Anthony Grafton's reflections on the Renaissance preoccupation with archeology, particularly the first chapter, "The Ancient City Restored: Archeology, Ecclesiastical History, and Egyptology," in his book *Bring Out Your Dead: The Past as Revelation* (Cambridge: Harvard University Press, 2001).

30 Juan Luis Vives, "Of the Mind," in *Introduction to Wisdom,* trans. Sir Richard Moryson, 1540. Quoted in *Vives: On Education: A Translation of the De Tradendis Disciplinis of Juan Luis Vives,* ed. and trans. Foster Watson (Cambridge: Cambridge University Press, 1913), xxxix.

the wise saw."[31] Students collected; teachers "shared," providing advice and moral truths by quoting authorities from the past. In Shakespeare's *Hamlet*, Laertes "characters" (copies) the precepts, Polonius recites them. According to Richard Harp,

> proverbs were part of the classical "Progymnasmata" or exercises (from Hermogenes' book of this title) of human-ist rhetorical education, where they, along with other aphoristic sayings and basic literary forms as fables, myths, episodes from history, legend, and the like were used in the development and refutation of theses.[32]

He continues:

> Proverbs which were stored in *florilegia*, (a compilation of extracts and maxims derived from the great writers of the past) could then be included among the memory devices contained in such collections call[ed] "cues for recollect-ing material read earlier" — the recalling of some particu-lar aphoristic poetical lines, for example, was the cue for remembering the whole context.[33]

If there is a position from which the speaker enacts a memo-rized proverb, it is from within a secreted, internalized book where the aphorism prefigures its articulation.

The tradition of proverb books flourished in the Renaissance through the sixteenth-century Reformation, with its keen fo-cus on the moral development of the student through *imitatio* and the inscription of maxims. English examples are replete. Thomas Elyot's *Bankette of Sapience* (1545) reads like a diction-

---

31 Rudolph Habenicht, "The Proverb Tradition in Early Sixteenth-Century," in his edited version of John Heywood's *A Dialogue of Proverbs* (Berkeley: Uni-versity of California Press, 1963), 9.

32 Harp, "Proverbs and Philosophy in *The Merchant of Venice* and *King Lear*," *Ben Jonson Journal* 16 (1995): 198 [197–215]. I am much indebted to Harp's reading, and his kind suggestions via email.

33 Ibid., 200.

ary of adages, with a table of contents, and organized with classical authors' names in the margins for quick referencing.[34] As the proverb tradition continues, the image of the wise "teacher" offering paternal advice in the form of moral dictums through adages becomes a cultural stereotype. John Heywood's *Dialogue of Proverbs* (1546) reflects on this trope and cleverly foregrounds these associative links in his domestic conduct book written as a polemic dialogue between an older man providing marital advice to a younger man.[35]

How to locate humanism's emphasis on rote education in the sweeping history of absolutism and economic changes that distinguish the sixteenth century? The use of common-placed adages and proverbs was at the heart of early modern Tudor humanism, where proverbs and other saws and maxims were the emphasis of rhetorical training. Up until quite recently, the histories of the Renaissance viewed this period as a moment of awakening from scripted habits of spiritual reflection. The task of Anthony Grafton and Lisa Jardine's authoritative corrective, *From Humanism to the Humanities: Education and the Liberal Arts in Fifteenth- and Sixteenth-Century Europe,* was to counter this narrative of secular cultivation.[36] Looking back, it is easy to see this book's analysis of humanism's larger politics informing much of the new historicist scholarship. Rather than see the growth of humanism in Europe in the last part of the fifteenth century as a progressive step toward intellectual enlightenment, Grafton and Jardine assert that the success of Renaissance humanism was not that it offered more intellectual freedom to readers of antiquity but that, as a conservative practice wedded to the aims of absolutism, it accommodated more the political

---

34 Elyot, Thomas, and Early English Books Online. *The Bankette of Sapience, Compyled By Syr Thomas Elyot Knyght, and Newly Augmented With Dyuerse Titles [et] Sentences* (London: Thomas Berthelet, 1542).

35 Heywood, *A Dialogue of Proverbs (1546),* ed. Rudolph Habenicht (Oxford: Oxford University Press, 1959).

36 Anthony Grafton and Lisa Jardine, *From Humanism to the Humanities: Education and the Liberal Arts in Fifteenth- and Sixteenth-Century Europe* (London: Duckworth, 1986).

necessities of the courts to produce the two traits of linguistic dexterity and political compliance to authority needed in its courtier-meritocracy class. Such an assessment paved the way for a critical remapping of these two traits not as a defining paradox of the times — one encouraging intellectual freedom, another a political pragmatism — or the combative ends of some simple political compass, but as something like the poles of a historically determined *Geist* where one reflex gets caught up in the oppositional dynamic of its other and informed by an op-positional logic. To speak in the most general terms, imagin-ing the reconciliation of this contradictory dialectic is perhaps still the legacy of historicist scholarship of the period, where it seems we emphasize one side of this spectrum over the other, where antiquity provides an exit from the world of pragmatism so that humanism's lure of the ancient world becomes an agent provocateur. The pagan literature of the past is here figured like an end in itself, providing a modicum of distance that lures the reader of classical literatures away like Marlowe's Faustus walk-ing off the stage with the promise of Helen's kiss. The other end of Grafton and Jardine's assessment emphasizes classicism as the bureaucratic language of absolutist statecraft. Think Spenser's Faerie Queen as the mirror image of Helen (nobody is going an-ywhere off stage, all pagan myth is merely an exercise in service to the Prince). The humanist performs as legal functionary of the state. This is the Foucauldian paradigm writ large of "power writing its subversion," the perspective that sees the revisionist humanist fantasy not as escape but of grafting any and all an-cient pagan myths to the Christian state as a celebration of the patron's power.

Readers of the adage today must make their way in this basic dialectic of critical options where the larger pattern of humanist educational reforms is seen to be informed by the cultural poli-tics of patronage. I think of Renaissance humanism's rote learn-ing as part of its intellectual legacy, but commonplacing (the act of reading for maxims to then write in one's tablet of memory) as the "practice" of this heritage in the every day world of the court. The commonplacing of books made the act of reading very much an intensely personal one, a memory work geared to the study for action, asking the reader to develop nuanced repertoires that, as time went on, became sophisticated discursive frameworks that shaped the readers ability to negotiate the politics of favor and rhetorical self-display. Proverbs uttered in a pithy and familiar form, placed artistically in an appropriate place in a speech or a play, "bring alive the traditional notion of the proverb as *iaculum*," Harp explains, "a dart or javelin, a weapon that can strike an opponent in a particular spot from a great distance."[37] Surely, to name such placement of proverbs in one's everyday speech a "javelin" gives one a sense of the performative nature of the speech act occurring within the competitive context of the Tudor court; humanism had as its political civic project that of service to the state. That is, the use of proverbs and adages are ideologically entwined with court culture, with its intense fascination with artistic self-presentation, a space where inserting conventional wisdom in the form of maxims and adages are at one with the courtier's aesthetic project of self-presentation through mimicry. By memorizing important "stock" lines across a range of themes, the gentleman can affect a series of tones and postures to accommodate the subtle play of pressures in the politics of favoritism of the court. "In this context," Harp suggests, "the proverb or maxim is the key to a knowledge that is hidden only in the sense of not being at hand or not written down in a readily available text but rather secreted away in the memory, where it could be 'found.'"[38]

Habits make for natural recall. Placing these adages in the mind, the student would come to them later, discover them in the recess of their imagination like tripping on an old stone, and ply them for practical use. In the late sixteenth and early seventeenth centuries, writers voiced anxieties about memory work as a perdurable practice for constructing stylized selfhood (think

---

37 Harp, "Proverbs and Philosophy," 199.
38 Ibid., 200.

Osric) and salvaging lost myths.[39] Scholars emphasize how humanists eventually became aware of the limits of scripted forms of rhetorical analysis. Rebecca Bushnell and Ann Moss have described the growing shift away from the mnemonic forms of imitation in writing.[40] Moss argues that the printed commonplace book died out in the seventeenth century when nature was set free from the shroud of ancient learning and the Aristotelian model of knowledge was supplanted by the empirical mode of inquiry codified by the new breed of gentleman scientists. "The commonplace-book was vulnerable," she explains, "and not only to new methods of enquiry and to a growing sense that evidence was empirically and scientifically measurable across a spectrum of probability. It also fell victim to a social code of polite behavior and to a consensual aesthetic of good taste which were inimical to its primary qualities of abundance and display; and its open ended acceptance of variety … was a potential irritant to a political culture centered on uniformity."[41]

But at its outset, the humanist program was codified through the publication of popular books like Erasmus's magnum opus, *Adagiorum Chiliades* (1508). It is widely considered the most influential text in the proverb tradition. It will help to understand the Renaissance version of the tsunami stone — or Radiation Cautionary Marker — to further analyze Erasmus's ideas of the adage. The proverb litters the Renaissance imaginary; they are strewn throughout the writing much like rocks in a field. To read from the period unaware of their placement is to ignore the signs for the trees, as it were. For the Renaissance humanist, the saws of ancient writers really did hold the wisdom of the past, revered truth carved in a form that outlives the

---

39 See Andrew Hiscock's discussion of the "memorial debate" in *Reading Memory in Early Modern Literature* (Cambridge: Cambridge University Press, 2011).

40 Rebecca Bushnell, *A Culture of Teaching: Early Modern Humanism in Theory and Practice* (Ithaca: Cornell University Press, 1996); Ann Moss, *Printed Commonplace-Books and the Structuring of Renaissance Thought* (Oxford: Clarendon Press, 1996).

41 Moss, *Printed Commonplace-Books,* 225–26.

countless tides. Much was invested in collecting and preserving them. In the following, I want to discuss in detail how Erasmus conceived of the adage. Erasmus meant to model this literacy practice by printing his collection as an ongoing project.[42] For Erasmus, the magical quality of proverb was that it preserved the ancient wisdom of the past in a fixed language, a monument that survives the storms of change. Renaissance humanism held as one of its principle fantasies the recovery of the lost wisdom of the ancients. To collect and disseminate this knowledge in the form of adages was Erasmus's life-long project, one to which he dedicated, as legend has it, two hours of every working day. Erasmus's popular book is a compendium of proverbs collected by the author throughout his adult life. The book's printing, in various editions, spanned Erasmus's career. It appeared in different printings, growing in length with each new edition. The first version, *editio princeps,* was printed in Paris in 1500, titled the *Collectanea,* a thin volume with only 818 proverbs. This first version, according to Margaret Phillips, went through 27 printings.[43] As it was being reprinted, Erasmus continued to add to it. In a kind of dizzying pattern of printing-leapfrog, this first version was still being sold as a new expanded version, titled *Adagiorum Chiliades,* was published by Aldine Press in Venice in 1508. The new *Adagiorum* contained 3,260 proverbs. Several editions were printed, the final version in 1533 containing over 4,200 adages. Because the book appeared in so many updated forms, with so many formal essays, biographical and cheeky self-references (his entry for "Make haste slowly," a full-length essay defending to his friends the purchase of his new and improved version, is considered a *tour de force* mock encomium), the book can be seen as Erasmus's great meta-textual book of hours, chronicling the humanist's first-hand encounter with his ancient authorities, his "bookmarking" of classical verities for fellow students of Greek and Latin. *Adagiorum* is one of the great models of

---

42 Desiderius Erasmus, *The Adages of Erasmus.*
43 Margaret Mann Phillips, *The "Adages" of Erasmus: A Study with Translations* (Cambridge: Cambridge University Press, 1964).

Renaissance humanist thought that demonstrate the peculiar fetish for cataloging and rote learning. Most importantly, it was a book that lived its promise of providing a window into the old world. "The book was a treasure house of style," Phillips explains, "[b]ut the essential aim was to recapture, in this handy portmanteau form, the outlook and way of life of the classical world, through its customs, legends, and social institutions, and to put within reach of a modern public the accumulated wisdom of the past."[44]

Erasmus made a point to cast a wide net in his definition of what counts as an adage. Erasmus included "proverbial metaphors" as part of his focus, for example, looking to define common experience — "generally familiar" forms of labor and daily life. "Generally speaking," Erasmus explains, "every aphorism approaches the genus proverb, and in addition metaphor and in particular allegory, and among these especially such as are taken from important fields which are generally familiar, such as seafaring and war."[45] The definition of what counts as a proverb rests more in its use than its "fit" within a rhetorical form.

Erasmus exhibits throughout his introduction a fascination for the way that common knowledge is learned, processed, and retained in the memorized form across a spectrum of social activities. It is an epistemic distinction important to the understanding of Erasmus's project. The true value of the proverb is that the metaphor absorbs and retains the localized memory of its making; there is a common task familiar to communal life inscribed in the very logic of the adage. In turn, this localized experience in one "field" is disseminated to those practicing other trades and is offered as an implied instruction manual — common wisdom — for practical application, a kind of tool kit of affective responses for ready employment. When defining what counts as a proverb in his introduction, then, Erasmus is defining a process of invention, how to "speak" proverbs, how to cast knowledge in stone:

44 Ibid., xiii.
45 Erasmus, *Adages,* 20.

Examples of these are: to sail with a following wind, to be shipwrecked, to turn one's sail about, to hold the tiller, to bale out the bilge-water, to spread one's sails to the wind and to take in sail … and hundreds of others of the same kind, which only need to be drawn out a little to assume the form of a proverb. In the same way there are those which are taken from well-known things and exceedingly familiar in everyday experience, as for instance whenever there is a transference from the physical to the mental, as turn the thumb down (to show support), to wrinkle one's brow (to take offense), etc.[46]

The adage is a magical transferring tool, one that sets the "the physical to the mental," and figures this knowledge for future use. In his "Literature as Equipment for Living," Kenneth Burke described the value of proverbs from a similar sociological perspective: "proverbs are designed for consolation or vengeance, for admonition or exhortation, for foretelling."[47] He continues:

Social structures give rise to "type" situations, subtle subdivisions of the relationships involved in competitive and cooperative acts. Many proverbs seek to chart, in more or less homey and picturesque ways, these "type" situations. I submit that such naming is done, not for the sheer glory of the thing, but because of its bearing upon human welfare.[48]

It was Burke's dream, in this embryonic essay, to imagine literature as "proverbs writ large," working to respond to social encounters: if "proverbs are strategies for dealing with situations," then why cannot we see different types of literary texts doing the same, to "take literature out of its separate bin and give it a place in a general 'sociological' picture."[49] In something of a prelude

46 Ibid.
47 Kenneth Burke, *The Philosophy of Literary Form: Studies in Symbolic Action* (New York: Vintage Books, 1941), 293.
48 Ibid., 294.
49 Ibid., 296.

to the structuralist turn, Burke imagines that "in so far as situations are typical and recurrent in a given social structure, people develop names for them and strategies for handling them."[50] What makes Burke's simple observation so striking is the way he imagines a presumed synchrony to the available options literary texts have to respond to these typical "situations" (this, in advance of Lévi-Strauss's publications by a few years). To get to this insight, Burke first postulates the proverb as a literary form whose specific "strategy" is to cope with affairs of life (he called proverbs "medicine"). "Here is realism for promise, admonition, solace, vengeance, foretelling, instruction, charting, all for the direct bearing that such acts have upon matters of welfare."[51]

One could respond that Burke's theory of the medicinal use of proverbs is foreshadowed by Erasmus (I have no evidence that Burke even read *Adagiorum Chiliades*), but it is probably more accurate to say that Erasmus's definition of the proverb as "strategy" makes Burke's observation more an elaboration, making twentieth-century pragmatism bear witness to its early modern roots. For Erasmus, the proverb was always a function of social welfare, part of the arsenal of humanist ethics kept vital and consistent through constant reiteration and application. Though offered in the medium of common speech, the adage is nonetheless the perfect portal to the ancient wisdom dreamt of by early modern humanism because it remains unchanged across time: "what vanishes from written sources, what could not be preserved by inscriptions, colossal statues and marble tables, is preserved intact in a proverb."[52] But at its outset, the proverb was presented by humanists as an elegant medium through which to accommodate Christian notions of collective spiritual experience.[53] In his *Adagiorum,* Erasmus equates proverbs with an ancient language of immanent knowledge "very similar to

50 Ibid., 297.
51 Ibid., 296.
52 Erasmus, *Adages,* 198.
53 Kathy Eden, *Friends Hold All Things in Common: Tradition, Intellectual Property, and the Adages of Erasmus* (New Haven: Yale University Press, 2001).

the rites of religion, in which things most important and even divine are often expressed in ceremonies."[54] There is "no form of teaching which is older than the proverb....What were the oracles of those wise old Sages but proverbs?" he asks. "They were so deeply respected in the old time," he continues "that they seemed to have fallen from heaven rather than to come from men....And so they were written on the doors of temples, as worthy of the gods; they were everywhere to be carved on columns and marble tablets as worth of immortal memory." It is no surprise that Erasmus fantasizes about the origin of his own humanism as a moment of transcription where divine knowledge is written on permanent stone surfaces. When thinking about the universality of proverbs he returns to this image:

> There is ... in these proverbs some native authentic power of truth. Otherwise how could it happen that we should frequently find the same thought spread abroad among a hundred peoples, transposed into a hundred languages, a thought which has not perished or grown old even with the passing of so many centuries, which pyramids themselves have not withstood?[55]

But having considered the idea of speaking to the future in the context of tragedy, real and imagined, we can see a new social function of the rote habits of Edgar's proverbial "Speak what we feel." Erasmus and his readers already imagined themselves walking across the plain of a fallen world, like figures in the EPA's imagined landscape of thorns. However, the early modern reader was better equipped when they encountered the ancient language offered on "archival paper in the information center" that was classical antiquity. Etched in the marble tablets of the mind, they had countless forms of sage advice equipping them for survival. "Man is a wolf to man," "Man is but a bubble," "To exact tribute from the dead," "To know a lion by his claws." In

54 Erasmus, *Adages,* 13.
55 Ibid., 16.

Erasmus's *Adagiorum,* each entry is followed by a quick genealogy of original sources, and a rough definition of the meaning
and value. Justifying the placement of adages in the whole of
the work, Erasmus defended them as thematic windows to the
greater work: "And, Pliny says, the miracle of nature is greater
in the most minute creatures, in the spider or the gnat, than in
the elephant, if only one looks closely; and so, in the domain
of literature, it is sometimes the smallest things which have the
greatest intellectual value."[56]

What we hear in many of these hollow proclamations in *Lear*
are characters pulling back from the present within their proverbial insertions. I want to turn now to Shakespeare's use of
proverbs.

Shakespeare's Proverbial Voice

> … know thou this, that men
> Are as the time is.
> — *King Lear* 5.3.31–2

> To plainness honor's bound,
> When majesty stoops to folly.
> — *King Lear* 1.1.148–49

Shakespeare inherited this mixed but vibrant humanist tradition. To situate Shakespeare's use of adages is a difficult task. Any
critic of his work must feel a bit apprehensive about unpacking
even the slightest aspect of his writing from the Gordian knot of
scholarship that binds it to various interpretive traditions. Situ-
ating Shakespeare's use of proverbs is such a "well worn path,"
Erasmus might say, in the legacy of scholarly themes.[57] (Or he

56 Ibid., 12.
57 The major scholarly works that focus on Shakespeare's use of proverbs are
    R.W. Dent, *Shakespeare's Proverbial Language: An Index* (Berkeley: Uni-
    versity of California Press, 1981), Morris Tilley, *A Dictionary of Proverbs
    in England in the Sixteenth and Seventeenth Century* (Ann Arbor: Univer-
    sity of Michigan Press, 1950), and F.P. Wilson, "The Proverbial Wisdom of

might think, "[N]o stone left unturned?") The critical analysis of Shakespeare's proverbial style is part of a longer critical tradition, the age-old fascination with Shakespeare as a "popular" poet whose familiarity with common idioms and figures of speech distinguish the decorum of his work.[58] Shakespeare was writing at a time when the highly ornate euphuistic style popular in the 1580s was slowly becoming outmoded and subject to ridicule.[59] The use of proverbs and *sententiae* to emphasize the authority of antiquity must be seen in the context of this other fashionable "humanist" literary style. It would be nice to separate out the different coded styles and assign their class orientations, where perhaps the use of common adages work as a cultural counter to a coded courtly style. But proverbial embellishments augmented the highly alliterative equipoise offered in Lyly's sentence. Take the interior monologue of the distraught Bellaria from Robert Greene's *Pandosto* as an example of how the proverbial style worked within the euphuism:

Thou seest now Bellaria, that care is a companion to honor, not to povertie, that high Cedars are crushed with tempests, when low shrubs are not touched with the winde: precious Diamonds are cut with the file, when despised pibbles lye safe in the sand. Delphos is sought to by Princes, not beggers: and Fortune's Altars smoke with king's presents, not with poore mens gifts. Happy are such Bellaria, that curse Fortune for contempt, not feare: and may wish they were, not sorrow they have been. Thou art a Princesse, Bellaria, and yet a prisoner; borne to the one by descent, assigned to

Shakespeare," in *Shakespearean and Other Studies* (Oxford: Clarendon Press, 1969).

58 For an overview of the controversy of Shakespeare as "popular," see Michael Bristol, "Theater and Popular Culture," in *A New History of Early English Drama* (New York: Columbia University Press, 1997), 231–51.

59 Though John Lyly's *Euphues: The Anatomy of Wit* (1578) was reprinted up to 1636, according to John Dover Wilson, it is typically seen to be the reigning style of the 1580s. The first signs of its "prodigal" excess is found in critiques as early as 1589. See John Dover Wilson, ed., *John Lyly* (New York: Haskell House, 1905), 58.

the other by dispite: accused without cause, and therefore oughtest to dye without care: for patience is a shield against Fortune, and a guiltlesse minde yeeldeth not to sorrow.[60]

Alone, dejected in her prison cell, Greene's heroine speaks to herself in an oddly affected manner. For modern readers, it is hard to imagine how such a mishmash of proverbial wisdom and breathless rhetorical posturing— "care a companion to honor not to poverty"— could offer succor to anyone in a lonely hour. Part of the aesthetic pleasure of reading Greene is this pompous play of narrative style, where the showmanship of the formal sentence gilds the recycled plots. The passage from Greene also allows us to think of another important aspect of the adage's placement in the cultural imaginary. At the moment where this inward subjectivity speaks (to herself) of her misery and desperation, it seems the austere proverbial phrase steps in to center the experience in a familiar perspective important for self-understanding. Bellaria's plodding euphuistic reflection on her imprisonment— "borne to the one by dissent, assigned to the other by despite"— seems to bolster the stoic acceptance of her lot. I want to come back to all of these issues below, but for now it is enough to mention that what appears a moment of rather staid rhetorical style is actually a violent, protracted scene of profound inwardness, where a volatile affective register is articulated through the communal voice. It provides a snapshot of early modern affective charge where intense emotional dynamism plays out against a background of proverbial phrases. We will return to this reflex in *Lear*.

When describing how Shakespeare "uses" proverbs, it is hard not to enter into a sustained critical discussion of his aesthetic, since what we regard as a recurring tendency will become the method that we identify as functioning in his writing. Generally, Shakespeare's use of proverbs is referential. That is, adages

---

60 Robert Greene, *Pandosto: The Triumph of Time,* in *Shakespeare's Library: A Collection of the Plays, Romances, Novels, Poems and Histories,* ed. William Hazlitt and John Collier, vol. 4 (London: Reeves and Turner, 1875), 33–4.

and proverbs are buried in wordplay or under layers of figurative association. Dexterous, exuberant, Shakespeare frequently exhibits too restless a linguistic energy to merely reproduce Erasmus's sententious voice like Greene, choosing rather to signal in different ways the proverb as a shared native knowledge. The proverbs are typically uttered free from citation (or quotation marks) as such, working more as evocative phrasing, metaphoric catalysts at work in the figurative language. Take as an example this line by Kent in the first act of *King Lear*. Defending Cordelia, Kent tells Lear to "check this hideous rashness" and reverse his decision:

> Answer my life my judgment,
> Thy youngest daughter does not love thee least;
> Nor are those empty-hearted whose low sounds
> Reverb no hollowness. (1.1.153–55)

Kent tells Lear he is misreading Cordelia's silence: her lack of words is not a sign of an empty heart. The line plays off the clever adage, "empty vessels sound most," a sixteenth-century version of "squeaky wheels get the grease." Kent is saying that Cordelia's heart is not "hollow" or empty, even though she refused to play the love test. By using the adage to begin with, Kent is reminding Lear that his other daughters are empty-hearted and their professions of love "reverb" from an empty hold. Shakespeare is not simply citing the adage, he folds it into dialogue, asking the audience to recall the maritime image. Lear is being reminded that he is *not* listening to the sage advice offered through the adage. Importantly, like with the scene from Greene above, this is a moment of striking affective display: Kent is proffering a proverb so that the King can reflect on his inner emotional state, to "police" his emotions from the calculated perspective offered through the wisdom of the adage. When we turn to *King Lear*, I want to investigate how this figurative proverb, working as it does through association, becomes more and more overtly "proverbial" or sententious.

I will call this type of easy allusion or reference to an adage, *embedded* proverb. Many of Shakespeare's proverbs appear as allusions to an implied proverbial saw, appearing as idiomatic phrases that advance the figurative wordplay. The discovery of a proverb at work in the general image of a line must have promised, for an era of twentieth-century textual scholarship, the magic box to exposing the poet's artistic process. The embedded proverb was seen to explain odd or quizzical phrasing that sometimes eluded scholars. Take, for example, the line of Kent's when tripping up the obsequious Oswald, "you base football player. [*Tripping up his heels*]" (1.4.74). R.W. Dent finds the line referring to the adage "All fellows at football never stand upon place."[61] This is almost too convenient of an explanation of a line that is sometimes footnoted as merely about class politics, but it's a good example of how an incidental turn of phrase might be conditioned by the popular adage.[62] It is a rather random thought insertion on Kent's part, elsewise. And the adage certainly explains the pratfall humor behind the stage direction. That said, I do believe that dramatists of the time used proverbs to signpost the general themes of their work. The best analysis of this sort is Richard Harp's "Proverbs, Philosophy, and Shakespeare's *The Merchant of Venice* and *King Lear*," which demonstrates how Shakespeare's clever use of proverbs accentuates the various perspectives of the characters: "Proverbs aid in not only illuminating philosophical conundrums but also in developing character."[63] "Revelation of character," he continues,

---

61 Dent, *Shakespeare's Proverbial Language,* 108–9.

62 If indeed this is the case with this line. Dent has only two other sources, but I have no reason to disbelieve his observation except the tradition of footnotes that accompany the edited text and explain this line about Kent's critique of Oswald's upstart position.

63 Harp, "Proverbs and Philosophy," 210. Harp's focus is on Shakespeare's elaboration of the themes of wisdom and "the praise of 'nothingness.'" Harp's idea of "proverbial compression" is extremely useful in thinking about how the proverbs in the play may have served as conceptual starting points for the author. See his analysis of Shakespeare's handling of the proverb, "nothing can be turned into nought" (208–9).

is rarely a simple matter in Shakespeare but ... the citing of familiar proverbs and their modification, which a modern audience might well miss, would have been a significant aid to Shakespeare's very mixed audience of rank and intelligence in following the dramatist's intricate and compressed character points.[64]

Even when making self-conscious use of the embedded proverb, we can nonetheless see Shakespeare sometimes working to elaborate or question the meaning of the original maxim. F.P. Wilson considers the most famous references to an adage in all of Shakespeare, Lady Macbeth's notorious reproach. It is another good example of an embedded proverb:

> Art thou afeard
> To be the same in thine own act and valour
> As thou art in desire? Wouldst thou have that
> Which thou esteem'st the ornament of life,
> And live a coward in thine own esteem,
> Letting "I dare not" wait upon "I would,"
> Like the poor cat i' the adage? (1.7.39–44)[65]

The adage is from "the cat would eat fish yet dare not wet its feet." Wilson makes mention of how the popularity of Shakespeare's reference outweighs (or outlasts) that of the adage, "today perhaps one in a thousand recognizes the adage and how apt it is to the occasion,"[66] and so the casual, "oblique" (Wilson's term) use of the proverb goes unnoticed. It's true that Lady Macbeth's spin on the adage is playfully intertextual, adding another figurative dimension to the image by splitting the cat into two allegorical sub-cats, "I dare not" and "I would," a feline psychomachia of doubt played out over a fishbowl.

---

64 Ibid., 210.
65 William Shakespeare, *Macbeth,* in *The Norton Shakespeare: Based on the Oxford Edition,* 2nd edn. (London: Norton, 2008).
66 Wilson, "The Proverbial Wisdom of Shakespeare," 146.

The other type of proverb is the overt or self-conscious citation (a visible use of adage) that appears to come with quotation marks around it. Shakespeare rarely has characters talking
about proverbs as such. Dent mentions the following example
in his definitive study when talking about Shakespeare's own
particular use of the word proverb; this exchange in *Henry V*
3.7 can serve as an excellent demonstration of how Shakespeare
is aware that proverbs are part of the game of rhetorical display.
The scene below is when the Constable of France unmasks the
Dauphin's self-deceit and inflated estimation of his abilities, "I
think he will eat all he kills." The Duke of Orleans makes a show
of defending the Dauphin:

> ORLEANS: I know him to be valiant.
> CONSTABLE: I was told that by one that knows him better than you.
> ORLEANS: What's he?
> CONSTABLE: Marry, he told me so himself; and he said he cared not
> who knew it.
> ORLEANS: He needs not; it is no hidden virtue in him.
> CONSTABLE: By my faith, sir, but it is; never any body saw it but his
> lackey. 'Tis a hooded valour; and when it appears, it will bate.
> ORLEANS: Ill will never said well.
> CONSTABLE: I will cap that proverb with "There is flattery in
> friendship."
> ORLEANS: And I will take up that with "Give the devil his due."
> CONSTABLE: Well placed: there stands your friend for the devil:
> have at the very eye of that proverb with "A pox of the devil."
> ORLEANS: You are the better at proverbs, by how much "A fool's
> bolt is soon shot."
> CONSTABLE: You have shot over.
> ORLEANS: 'Tis not the first time you were overshot. (3.7.93–112)[67]

Here Shakespeare uses common adages to amplify the tension
between these two men, but also to complicate the use of pro-

---

67 William Shakespeare, *Henry V,* in *The Norton Shakespeare: Based on the Oxford Edition,* 2nd edn. (London: Norton, 2008).

verbial speech in a play about the politics of expressing alliance or friendship in the court. In the margins of this scene is the history of humanist education, as discussed by Grafton and Jardine, shifting to accommodate the new court, where diplomacy and rhetorical legerdemain will prove more valuable assets for the courtier than the martial arts. The Duke's mastery of proverbs may win the day, but the audience is left wondering if the superfluous wordplay isn't one with the Dauphin's court of flattery, hyperbole, and effete narcissism. Is the Duke buying into the Dauphin's self-image? Defending him out of a sense of friendship? Perhaps the Constable has a point in giving the devil his due. In a play that is guarded in its celebration of a Machiavellian prince who succeeds by renouncing his pals and performing the prince, this scene foregrounds the theme of using proverbial language to expose and cover up one's fealty to power.

I want to now move to an analysis of proverbs in Shakespeare's *King Lear*. To place Shakespeare's *King Lear* in the context of this history of humanist education, one notes that the use of proverbs and maxims is at one with the nostalgic tone of the play in its glance back to England's pagan past. Given that the humanist tradition of using proverbs was slowly waning when Shakespeare begins to write his plays, the appearance of what I am calling the proverbial voice should be seen as one among many of his cues to signal a sense of nostalgia. In a tragedy that retells the old legend of England's ancient king, Shakespeare employs proverbs to effect many types of attitudes toward history and character in this incredibly skeptical play. It is as if Shakespeare follows Erasmus's advice by using proverbs to inhabit his medieval subjects, making his characters speak like stone tablets from the past.

CHAPTER TWO

Lear and the Proverbial Reflex

> Good king, that approve the common saw,
> Thou out of heaven's benediction comest
> To warm the sun!
> …Nothing almost sees miracles
> But misery.
> — *King Lear* 2.2.153–55

> For the [proverb] names a particular action event of
> experience: it lends it a familiarity in advance, *avant
> la lettre*; we may even say that the process for naming
> which is at one with the very category of the definite
> article as such constructs its object and creates the first
> familiarities, the first organized recognitions as those
> become sedimented in language.
> — Fredric Jameson, *Brecht and Method*[1]

Proverb as Voice: Coining Affective Responses

Proverbs speak from a placeless time before. In the passage
above from Act 2, Kent is bewailing his condition as he is newly
shackled in the stocks by Cornwall for his violent treatment of
Oswald. Kent begins his speech by saying that the King's condition, having just deposed himself and being denied his train of
followers by his daughter, proves true the common adage, "Out
of heaven's benediction to warm the sun." Shakespeare signals
through this reference to the popular adage, "Out of God's bless-

---

1   Fredric Jameson, *Brecht and Method* (New York: Verso, 2011), 132.

ing into the warm sun" (out of heaven and into the heat of the sun), that Lear's fall is anticipated by a common story known to all. Kent is reading the plot for the audience. He is placing the king's story as a parable common to all, recording it through the witness of the adage. Kent freezes time in language, giving us a picture of Lear's actions as tableaux. As the play progresses, the use of proverbs to record and bear witness to catastrophe is amplified as the shift in focus moves from the embedded adage to the citational.[2] In this chapter, I want to analyze more closely the use of proverbial speech in *King Lear*. We are in a position to see rote language as more than an artificial or a trivial form of knowing. What complicates the use of adage in this play is that its central thematic focus on forgiveness is told through the story of a king who trusts too much in the courtly "scripted" forms of devotion and duty. Put simply, while its villains practice deceit through rhetorical dissembling, those who are the targets of this deceit speak to themselves in a no less scripted language to make sense of their plight. The artifice of rhetorical speech is the *pharmakon* within the play, both the poison and medicine to its alienated characters. Lear's progress from king to beggar on the heath can be read as a cautionary story about trusting one mode of (mediated, rehearsed) rote speech over another. When characters recoil from violence and speak the blank voice of proverbs, Shakespeare is weighing the limits of the humanist rhetorical imagination. How to read this move to the proverbial, then, and what are the deeper critical implications today if we abandon the idea that the play is not distancing us from mediated forms of consciousness but pointing to them in positive terms?

Up to this point, we have been considering the adage as a maxim born from experience. What would it mean to see proverbial speech as something one could mimic or perform? This

---

2   The idea of citational speech as a performative speech act is elaborated in William Worthen's *Shakespeare and the Force of Modern Performance* (Cambridge: Cambridge University Press, 2003). See also David Schalkwyk's "Text and Performance, Reiterated: A Reproof Valiant or Lie Direct?" *Shakespearean International Yearbook* 10 (2010): 47–76.

is not to discount the idea of inheriting proverbs from the past, but to broaden the idea of proverbs as a mode of speech that conjures a new mode of consciousness, "brings into existence" a special historical awareness of our existence. The quality of this form of historical reflection derives from the seeming universal circulation of the proverb. F.P. Wilson summed up the yeoman's task of accounting for proverbs as a kind of cultural ethnography relying mostly on scholarly hunches of an assumed commonality: "The editor of an historical dictionary is forced to ask, 'In common use when, and in what circles, and how common?', questions it is not always easy to answer."[3] This can be read as a secularization of Erasmus's own quizzical definition of the divine "origins" of the proverb. Their appearance seems magical. But the trace of their popularity is everywhere. What makes the two scholarly compendiums of Shakespeare's proverbs, Morris Tilley's 1950 *Dictionary of Proverbs in England in the Sixteenth and Seventeenth Century* and R.W. Dent's 1981 *Shakespeare's Proverbial Language: An Index,* so astounding is their groundwork into this implied common language.[4]

For the historian, the mystery of the proverb is, finally, that we don't know from where or when they derive. Speaking of any given saw or adage, we will never know who coined it or exactly how many people were familiar with it. Moreover, the belief that proverbs live forever, too, is a shaky idealism, considering some of them are predicated on arcane practices. So when hearing adages like "he must be either dead or teaching school" (which is not about skipping an academic conference), without knowing of the practice of using captured Greek soldiers as language teachers, the metaphor is lost to the storehouse of quaint relics. This is the contradiction at the heart of scholarly approaches to the proverb as enshrined *sententiae,* where it seems like schol-

---

3   F.P. Wilson, "The Proverbial Wisdom of Shakespeare," *Shakespearean and Other Studies* (Oxford: Oxford University Press, 1969), 145.

4   Morris Tilley, *A Dictionary of Proverbs in England in the Sixteenth and Seventeenth Century* (Ann Arbor: University of Michigan Press, 1950); R.W. Dent, *Shakespeare's Proverbial Language: An Index* (Berkeley: University of California Press, 1981).

arly habit trumps caution and lights on the topic much like the bold raven on the scarecrow. Busy counting the patterns of repetitions and allusions, it is easy to put aside doubts of evidence or the hollow stuff of one's perch. In part, the profundity of aphoristic discourse is to blame for the sound of the proverb's sagacity and seeming prevalence. Proverbs could be said to exist in the shadowy forest of *langue* in this way — the unsaid but governing principle of a known parlance — and come to us, as Erasmus assumed, "from the heavens." But this is a simple projection of their iterative quality: the sense that the proverb lived a life before its utterance. When Erasmus muses that they are given divinely he is fantasizing about the illusory origins of the proverb that appear *ex nihilo* from an indeterminate past, made visible through their trace, by constant evocation through Quintilian, Pindar, or Horace. But maybe what really sanctifies the utterance is not so much that ancient authorities used them but that they evoke a common experience that invites us to glimpse everyday life as a collective species. In this way, Erasmus can be said to actively construct an ideology of the proverb, a kind of Renaissance "strategic mysticism" that makes sacramental his own humanist practice of proverbial inscription as a kind of "tool-making" ritual that names specific social practices common to all. His collection is as much a handbook for coining the proverb — invoking and creating this sense of communal — as it is for collecting. To reflect on the immediate experience in such an aphoristic voice is to capture concrete experience of a specific encounter and preserve it, placing knowledge of one's affective response to the environment in a linguistic time capsule that survives for future communities.

To consider the proverb from this new perspective, we must think of it as a linguistic act with its own performative function. Kent is using citational proverbs to universalize or make common Lear's loss of privilege. The affective function of articulating this experience helps him understand his own condition by framing it in a common adage, what psychologists call a "dissonance-reducing mechanism."[5] Even if we have not heard the proverb before, we feel that we have. It *sounds* like something that could be passed around as a common moralism, like my scarecrow allusion above. It uses a given rustic setting and imparts wisdom shrouded in parable form. An allegory is suggested through its image of the historian repressing the questionable value of its certitude as a straw perch. And since it is articulated as an already established common view, questions that get to the heart of the proffered wisdom go unchecked: the raven is a historian of saws, but what is the scarecrow again? A straw man? A perch of scholarly method? Or an ineffective warning to think about one's sources? Part of the magic of the proverb is that they do this very important work of "sweeping under the rug" cognitive dissonance and meddling doubt. Questions we should have, on the face of it, are glossed in the very structure of the proverb's certitude; "no bees, no honey,"[6] is a popular adage from Sappho, so we're told by Erasmus, about the value of an unquestioned work ethic, and perhaps comes to us with added irony today (I imagine it will have an entirely different meaning in a few years if honey bees are not saved from extinction). Questions about how and when bees became stereotypes of faithful labor are begged in its articulation. Or why we need to work tirelessly for the same old honey. The glossing of epistemological categories is the special power of the proverb, the shrouding in aura of its object.

Now we are getting closer to understanding how some proverbs work to manage intersubjective trauma, how they work to

5   According the argument, the importance or seriousness of a "dissonant element" is reduced through the vocalization of the proverb. Daniel Stalder, "The Power of Proverbs: Dissonance Reduction through Common Sayings," *Current Research in Social Psychology* 15.7 (2010): http://www.uiowa.edu/~grpproc/crisp/crisp15_7.pdf. See also L. Simon, J. Greenberg, and J. Brehm, "Trivialization: The Forgotten Mode of Dissonance Reduction," *Journal of Personality and Social Psychology* 68 (1995): 247–60; and D.R. Stalder and P.G. Devine, "Why does social comparison reduce dissonance?" *Journal of Social and Personal Relationships* 29.3 (2012): 302–23.

6   Desiderius Erasmus, *The Adages of Erasmus,* ed. William Barker (Toronto: University of Toronto Press, 2001), 6.

provide a range of affective "scripts" for coping with different material realities: stress to social bonds, privation, physical violence, "necessity's sharp pinch." As in Kent's lines above, characters in *King Lear* appear to speak to themselves in a different voice, as if offering sage advice "through" the source of communal perspective. In this way, the proverbial voice can be seen to offer a secreted book of conditioned responses through which the speaking subject can monitor and adjust their position to their world. I want to argue that *King Lear* is a tragedy about faith in memorized language as a tool for survival, and as we'll see, it attempts to piece through the subtle philosophical differences between rote speech as both a form of blindness and insight, ethical impairment and linguistic subsistence. What follows in this chapter is a thematic reading of this contradiction. I want to point briefly to the context of eco-materialist aesthetic theory as I go, but I will return to speak about these broader theoretical concerns in the next chapter.

The proverbial reflex is typically interpreted via modernist theories of art. When a character like Kent uses a common adage to make sense of the King's fall (and perhaps his own condition in the stocks), it is sometimes seen a moment of profound irony, where a character expresses belief in divine retribution in the face of awful human cruelty or injustice. Say what he might, he is still, finally, sitting in the stocks. Consider Jonathan Dollimore's theory that these moments offer a "refusal of closure." He is looking at Edgar's lines about his father:

> The gods are just, and of our pleasant vices
> Make instruments to plague us:
> The dark and vicious place where thee he got
> Cost him his eyes. (5.3.170–73)

Dollimore explains the accounting of justice in these lines as a moment of alienation:

> Thus is responsibility displaced; but perhaps Edgar is meant
> to wince as he says [such lines] since the problem of course

is that he is making his society supernaturally intelligible at the cost of rendering the concept of divine justice so punitive and "poetic" as to be, humanly speaking, almost unintelligible.[7]

It is easy to hear skepticism behind Edgar's lines: he is speaking to his brother Edmund, the "instrument" referred to in the line, about his father's blindness and death. It is also easy to see how the lines work to make visible Edgar's belief in divine justice. For Dollimore, finally, it's a moment where the audience is distanced from Edgar's belief system, where the text motivates a level of self-conscious awareness. Shakespeare, it is argued, draws attention to two incompatible worlds: the idealism of the utterance and the stark reality of the world that conditions such a response. The critical frame presupposes that these moments in the text work as meta-commentary about ideology, on the effect of ideology to "mask" reality from the subject, and such meta-awareness encourages the audience to see the false consciousness at work in daily life. Dollimore's brilliant and succinct reading of the play is paradigmatic of a materialist approach, and though others offer a slightly different focus on what is being demystified, precisely — here it is Christian faith generally, "divine justice" — it articulates a basic attitude shared by many critics that aligns Shakespeare's skepticism with the modernist aesthetic operation of triggering rational self-awareness.[8] We have inherited this critical frame from modernism, I would argue, and with it, an implicit view of textual dissonance and concomitant Enlightenment ethics of literary pedagogy. But what if the process of uttering the words, the physical process of speaking in the proverbial voice, works on another level? An affective level to salve the wounds of necessity's sharp pinch? In the follow-

7   Jonathan Dollimore, *Radical Tragedy: Religion, Ideology, and Power in the Drama of Shakespeare and his Contemporaries* (Chicago: Chicago University Press, 1984), 203.

8   Dollimore's approach is representative of an older materialist approach that employs an Althusserian model to read art's demystification of ideologies ("systems of representations").

ing I want to unpack these moments of proverbial reflection in
King Lear and explore how they function affectively to position
characters in relation to their environment. Like many materialist approaches to the play, Dollimore imagines Shakespeare as a
kind of Brecht, using *ostranenie* (defamiliarization) to forestall
our entry into the faith behind Edgar's lines so that the audience
"sees" his idealism as wooden and flat. But what would it mean
to see this speech as a retreat into *progymnasmata*? Within the
old materialist frame, art is meant to estrange life, to shock us
out of this habituated existence. At first glance, Shakespeare's
King Lear seems to reverse the terms of this process: as the "nor-
mal" world is so violent, characters seem to cling to habituated
forms of speech to survive. But many questions follow: How
does the repetitive use of linguistic phrases and catch-terms
shape this process? How might this scripted identity work as a
site of retreat for the conscious mind?

I can begin by asking, is it even possible to read Shakespeare
free from a modernist paradigm?[9] Why jettison this model? I
will say at the outset that it might be impossible to do so, as the
critical methods we use are so ingrained and the assumptions so
much a part of the critic's tool world as to be nearly intractably
fixed in the very questions we ask of the text. In a manner that
Erasmus might say draws us back upstream, tracing how the
modernist perspective shapes our view of Shakespeare means
rethinking literary influence. "The springs of the sacred rivers
flow backwards," Erasmus would say. In this case, considering
how Shakespeare is read after or downstream of modernism,
going upstream means inverting our view of Shakespearean
tragedy coming before and anticipating modernity. What if
modernism comes before, in the sense that modernist theories

9　Charles Edelman's clever "Shakespeare and the Invention of the Epic Theater: Working with Brecht," in *Shakespeare Survey* 58 (2005): 130–36, plays
with the absurdist position parodied in David Lodge's *Small World: An Academic Romance* (New York: Penguin, 1995) about T.S. Eliot's influence on
Shakespeare; in Edelman's case, he discusses how Shakespeare gets his idea
of epic theater from Brecht. The point is, we read Shakespeare downstream
of Brecht, and see Brecht in his work.

of art and subjectivity shape the way we read early modern literature? Surely the Renaissance had its own equivalent aesthetic of ideological distancing?[10] It is not an overstatement to say we read Shakespeare through the grid of modernism and impose its sensibility onto his plays. This is to assert the perspectivalist handsaw that the reading subject always imposes his or her set of controlling assumptions on the text. Getting to Shakespeare's *King Lear* means wading through modernism first. In the lines above, Edgar is speaking in the proverbial key. He articulates his dread with the word through a citational proverb: "Pleasant vices / Make instruments to plague us." Who is speaking? Not a single subject, but a shared one. These lines are "haunted" by the citational quality of expression, an objectivism that bars Edgar entrance to a defeating anguish. Shakespeare is conscious of retrieving the legend of *King Lear* from the very beginning of medieval histories, and the characters seem to bare the trace of their origins as iconic figures of Saxon lore. Maynard Mack has commented that when compared to his other tragedies, Shakespeare's *King Lear* features characters who make quick decisions free from premeditated process. "Their acts," he observes, "have consequences but little history … Choice remains in the forefront of the argument … its psychic antecedents have been so effectively shrunk down in this primitivized world that ac-

10 The value of Hugh Grady's *Shakespeare, Machiavelli, and Montaigne: Power and Subjectivity from Richard II to Hamlet* (Oxford: Oxford University Press, 2002) is to map out this early modern aesthetic in terms recognizable to contemporary materialist historicism. The argument is that Shakespeare acquires an idea of political critique from Machiavelli and later from Montaigne. Another path to Shakespeare's theory of art's "distance" from ideology can be found in the body of scholarship that analyzes classical stoicism as the context to early modern drama's radical exposure of faith as an ideology. See Jamey Graham's "Consciousness, Self-Spectatorship, and Will to Power: Shakespeare's Stoic Conscience," *English Literary Renaissance* 44.2 (2104): 24–74, but also the many formative works in this area: Earl Miner, "Stoic Reading in Renaissance English," *PMLA* 86 (1971): 1029–30; Audrey Chew's *Stoicism in Renaissance English Literature* (New York: Peter Lang, 1988); Gilles D. Monsarrat's *Light from the Porch: Stoicism and English Renaissance Literature* (Paris: Didlier Erudition, 1984).

tion seems to spring directly from the bedrock of personality."[11] Mack notes that this bedrock of character shapes action as a foregone conclusion: "We feel no imaginable psychological process could make Kent other than loyal, Goneril other than cruel, Edgar other than 'a brother noble.'"[12] One of the uncanny effects of a fully realized world populated with historical archetypes — automata of written predispositions — is that characters must experience their actions only in the context of memory, defending past choice without the language to proffer options, as if suffering from chronic short-term memory loss. "I know I did this (history says it's so), but how did I get here?" As a realist character with rational thought, they now have to explain past actions as conscious acts free from the deliberative process that produced them. The effect is rather like that of using shapes from a tableau to inhabit a landscape rendered in three-point perspective. Often characters share these inward thoughts on the meaning of these past events in a hollow voice true to a more primitive form of proverbial inscription, speaking in a way that stands out against the backdrop of unfolding narrative. Kent reflects on his situation in the stocks, and he is given to placing his lot against the homiletic frame: "Ahh, nothing almost sees miracles / But misery" (2.2.157–58). Likewise, in a painful moment of dolorous reflection, Edgar's words are meant to frame his father's blindness and death, but also to provide a way to articulate his grief and mollify inner wounds by speaking from a shared text of allegory. His is a sorrow now shared without solitude. To make sense of his inwardness according to a realist sense of angst or alienation might be to force his voice to blend with the social realist dimension of the play. But at what cost? Dollimore himself offers his Brechtian analysis as something of a guess to the curiously stoic tone of these lines: "*perhaps* Edgar is wincing," he says.

11 Maynard Mack, *King Lear in Our Time* (Berkeley: University of California Press, 1972), 93.

12 Ibid.

In his analysis of Bertolt Brecht's "method," Fredric Jameson accounts for the modern playwright's penchant for using proverbs. Jameson's is a good starting point for this chapter because he is thinking about how proverbs seem to echo from a self-made well of ancient wisdom. Jameson's theoretical account of the proverb will help us define its recurring use in *King Lear*. "When we our betters see bearing our woes, / We scarcely think our miseries our foes" (3.6.95–96). "Our means secure us, and our mere defects / Prove our commodities" (4.1.21–22). Such aphorism seems carved out of the proverbial terrain of the narrative. Brecht (refracted through Jameson) is a good starting point because Brecht was known to coin proverbs, to affect a proverbial wisdom, in scenes from his plays. Jameson is puzzled by Brecht's use of proverbial speech because as a dramatist and critic, Brecht's work is known for inaugurating the modernist drama with its various shocks to modern habituated existence, art as a no-holds-barred war against any and all domesticated views of reality. Brecht's name is coterminous with the various techniques associated with drama's ability to rattle us out of complacency: distancing effects, estrangement, alienation, dissociation. Yet here is an artist sympathetic to proverbial speech whose universalizing language runs counter to the technique of distancing perspective. Why does Brecht favor the proverb at all? And how does he use it? It seems, on the face, an example of aesthetic oil and water.[13]

Jameson begins by positing that the proverb grounds experience in absolute categories:

For the definite article names a particular action event of experience: it lends it a familiarity in advance, *avant la*

13 There is a bit of tentativeness in Jameson's definition of the proverb; he admits as much, saying, "I believe that it has to do with ...," in *Brecht and Method*, 132. Jameson wants to show Brecht setting up a commonsense perspective through proverbs that must later be defamiliarized: "we have seen it the deeper vocation of estrangement to undermine" (ibid.), but then moves to argue this is merely a stage we must move beyond to see proverb working to "de-reify" unknown proletariat experience.

lettre; we may even say that the process for naming which is at one with the very category of the definite article as such constructs its object and creates the first familiarities, the first organized recognitions as those become sedimented in language.[14]

Jameson fathoms that the proverb positions text and reader alike in a static world of origins: the use of the "the definite article opens up some Ur-perspective of a linguistic past of the verbally archaic," he explains,

the beginnings of time, the organization of the world into names and familiar categories. And it also seems to project those categories initially, and against all ideologies of contemporary linguistics, in the form of substantives. The definite article thus grounds Aristotelianism in the first habits of language itself, rather than in that process-oriented movement which philosophy has had painfully to recover after the long reign of Aristotelian common-sense."[15]

Jameson's definition is nearly coterminous with Erasmus's view of the proverb as a portal to an ancient wisdom, an "Ur-language," but the emphasis now is on the structure of the proverb as a *performative act,* a gesture that reproduces the sense of intuited truth free from the process of experience and reason, making actions substantive "things" of a recognizable world.

If the new eco-materialist theory asks that we see the emphasis on subjective self-awareness (and its insistence on the phenomenological horizon, the so-called "correlationism" leveled at Kantian philosophy) implicated in an even vaster form of ontological blindness and separation of the (other) objects of the world, then too we have to rethink the critical attitude toward

14 Ibid.
15 Ibid.

textual awareness.[16] The modernist theory of art "shocking" the viewer out of its somnambulant state takes as its starting point the idea that empirical awareness of one's social condition is not only possible, but necessary for self-guided agency. But surely this also presumes that waking up and seeing our "real" state will help manage our existence and further our survival, right? Who is this theory of art directed at precisely? Edgar? The audience of Edgar's pain? Or take the human audience as a baseline "referent." Does it help an individual subject suffering from the institutionalized neglect of poverty and the thousand privations associated with underclass existence to wake up and "see" their plight? Would it help a real homeless person to know they are functioning within an alienated ideological mindset? Such a question seems so absurd it's almost difficult to ask; or at least it seems so difficult to articulate because so much of our literary pedagogy takes as its starting point the "freedom" of the reader through critique, literature as a vehicle for ideological demystification.[17] At the very least, to insist that modernist theory of art might help such an individual seems goofy if not predicated on its own pathological displacement of discursive investments.

16 See the critique of correlationism in Quentin Meillassoux, *After Finitude: An Essay on the Necessity of Contingency,* trans. Ray Brassier (London: Continuum Press, 2008), and developed in Ian Bogost, *Alien Phenomenology, or What It's Like To Be A Thing* (Minneapolis: Minnesota University Press, 2012).

17 And let's not assume that I am advancing the opposite: promoting an alienating false consciousness. Rather, the modernist theory itself seems to begin with this false binary, and I am teasing out a third term, what Greimas might identify as its "complementary contrary" of defamiliarization. In Greimas and Rastier, "The Interaction of Semiotic Constraints," *Yale French Studies* 41 (1968): 86–105. See Jacques Rancière's description of the problem of defining critique in the post-critical age in his *Emancipated Spectator* (London: Verso, 2011). For Rancière, critique is forestalled by the fact that "right-wing frenzy of post-critical thought and left-wing melancholy" collude. "Left wing melancholy invites us to recognize that there is no alternative to the power of the beast [global capitalism, elsewhere described as the "democratic thirst for egalitarian consumption"] and to admit we are satisfied with it. Right wing frenzy warns us that the more we try to break the power of the beast, the more we contribute to its triumph" (40).

Returning to Edgar's lines above, can we hear him speaking to himself as if he is recalling the cautionary markers in the landscape of thorns? Would it help him to know his father died for no purpose? At least part of the pain of this scene stems from the fact that this is precisely what we see. But the question is whether we want Edgar to see it. We can ask, then, how might the proverb be allowing him to survive the moment? Applying a new materialist theoretical sensibility to the play's representation of ruined nature requires that we rethink the rationalist premise of our application of modernist interpretive frameworks.

The Cynicism of Rhetorical Vestments

> The art of our necessities is strange,
> And can make vile things precious.
> — *King Lear* 3.2.70–71

While *King Lear* stages moments where characters speak through objective aphorism, the play begins with an analysis of the corrosive effects of rhetorical speech as concealment. Those who practice the oily art, as it is described by Cordelia, "speak and purpose not" (1.1.226). Commemorative speech defines the first acts of the play. If Shakespeare read *King Leir* (printed 1605, performed in 1594 by the Queen's and Lord Sussex's Men), along with the other versions of the legend, he was influenced by this play's emphasis on Ragan and Gonorill's deliberate plot to trick their father.[18] Jealous of Cordella's beauty and popularity, the two

18 Of the various sources for the *King Lear* legend, including Raphael Holinshed's *Chronicles of England, Scotland and Ireland* (1577), *Mirror for Magistrates* (Higgins version, 1574), Sidney's *Arcadia* (Book 2 Chapter 10, focusing on the Gloucester subplot), none emphasize the theme of flattery so ostensibly as the anonymous play *King Leir*. For edited versions of Holinshed, Higgins, and Sidney as they pertain to Shakespeare's *Lear*, see Vincent F. Petronella's edited Evans Shakespeare *King Lear* (Boston: Wadsworth, 2012). Geoffrey Monmouth calls *King Lear* "credulous," in his response to the daughters' fairytale responses to the king's question, but this does not fixate

sisters speak about their plans to trip her up. "Some desperate medicine must soon be applied," Ragan says, "To dim the glory of her mounting fame." Right after, they are told by the courtier Skalliger that the King plans to marry them off to suitors and to "be resolved of [his] tormenting doubt" "which of you three do bear most love to him." Ragan responds: "O that I had some pleasing Mermaid's voice, / For to enchant his senseless senses with!" Gonorill explains: "I will so flatter with my doting father, / As he was n'er so flattered in his life."[19] In this earlier version of the play, a strong emphasis is placed on these deceiving daughters' deliberate use of flattery as a means to secure the undue reward of a doting father. If we listen, we can hear Shakespeare returning to this earlier popular play. Shakespeare downplays the contest of flattery in the beginning of his narrative. We hear Goneril and Regan performing in their speeches, but we are not witness to any discussion in advance. In his version, the king announces the plan of the love test seemingly from nowhere, tripping on the idea as a way to "shake all cares and business from [his] age" (1.1.37). He is not the dupe of his daughter's precipitated trick. The effect of this change is to make the king an agent to his own fall: Lear's weakness stems from the moral blindness and an exaggerated faith in the ability to speak earnestly in the court. As Mack suggests, we're not privy to the reasons behind the characters' choices. The cautionary theme of flattery is the palimpsest of Shakespeare's focus on social dissolution: we hear it in silences of the play, as it were, surfacing when the king expresses anger and belated regret from the vantage point of the credulous gull of the 1605 play. In Shakespeare the excised scene of being tricked nonetheless still shapes the king's later angst, where Lear's anger seems curiously histrionic. Perhaps this explains why, in Shakespeare's *Lear*, in the epiphanal scenes of the

on their intentional deceit as much as the 1605 play. *History of the Kings of Britain*, ed. Sebastian Evans (London: J.M. Dent, 1904).

19 *King Leir*, "Precursors of Shakespeare Plays," at *Elizabethan Authors*, transcribed by Barboura Flues, ed. Robert Brazil, http://www.elizabethanauthors.org/king-leir-1605-1-16.htm, 2.60–80. Further quotations cited parenthetically within the text.

king's self-exploration there is an oddly refracted quality to the hyperbolized language about duplicity; at times these lines seem to echo from the structuring absence of this earlier play. Shakespeare's Lear never quite gets to the point of forgiving Goneril and Regan, but the hero of the 1605 *Leir* speaks of them first before getting to the moment of regret with Cordella:

> O, let me warn all ages that ensueth,
> How they trust flattery, and reject the trueth.
> Well, unkind Girls, I here forgive you both,
> Yet the just heavens will hardly do the like. (24.56–60)

In the 1605 *Leir,* forgiveness is expressed as a cautionary pronouncement against flattery. Shakespeare's Lear will not get off the hook so easily, and the just heavens will rain on everyone regardless. Shakespeare removes this moment from the king's story (a nodal point repressed in his revision of the play, I would argue) and turns the screw the other direction: Goneril and Regan will undo themselves in their reckless pursuit of Edmund's attention, and when they die, their stories seem to barely deserve our attention. When their bodies are brought on stage, the audience may identify with Albany's lines: "[T]his judgment of the heavens, that makes us tremble, / Touches us not with pity" (5.3.230–31). In one of the only moments of poetic justice, we are not allowed to feel its recuperative effect because at this exact moment we still await the messenger to see if Cordelia has survived Edmund's murder plot. Shakespeare's tragic hero never speaks from this lucid vantage point of moral insight with the ascribed power of affirming providential justice. Shakespeare calibrates this image of moral "preaching" as one subject to the indifferent powers of nature, not of one who boasts of its intent: "The first time we smell the air, / We wail and cry. I will preach to thee. Mark" (4.6.173–74).

If *King Lear* stages moments where characters live the rote self through the mnemonic language offered in proverbial wisdom, the tragedy is carving this cautionary path back to learned modes of speech by weighing it against courtly rhetoric as stylized dissembling. In the later acts of *King Lear,* the king's madness is shaped by a special preoccupation with the idea of a deceitful exterior that masks a true intent. Speaking honestly free from the trappings of rhetorical display is a leitmotif in Shakespeare's later plays with deep roots in Elizabethan culture of social mobility.[20] I want to briefly underscore this point here and offer a quick summary of the metaphysics of language as an exterior fashion of the self. It is easy to ignore the importance of this idea of rhetorical dissembling in *King Lear* because Lear's thoughts about his downfall are so histrionic, written with such grand strokes and set against broad philosophical and political backdrops, criticism cannot help but follow the lead of the poetic forays into cosmic decay, the disintegration of providentialism, patriarchal fantasies of social hierarchy and the Reform logic of unveiling iconoclasm and superstitious practices. Nevertheless, the initial unraveling of this world begins with people lying in ways that are not only socially permissible but culturally ordained. Put simply, as King Lear becomes mad, he becomes more and more obsessed with who is honest and who isn't. The belief that there is an unseen truth that sits under the social demands of accommodating one's speech to social encounters "writes" the king's madness, many of his later psychotic ramblings revealing this preoccupation with rhetorical deception. The image of a rhetorically dressed intent hidden under an outward speech is the initial source of Lear's cathected anger, as he displaces the conundrum of "speaking true" onto other characters and objects. His outbursts revolve around images of deceit inherent in "perjury" and "covert … seeming." Moreover, the vocabulary of Lear's guilt reproduces the hermeneutic of reading or unveiling the (latent) fallen nature clothed in artificial speech: "[T]hrough tattered clothes small vices do appear," he exclaims (4.6.168). Moreover, when Lear later rants on the heath about corrupt nature and dissolution of the flesh — "ruined pieces of nature" — he is always expressing this in the context of "feel-

20 Rosemary Kegl, *The Rhetoric of Concealment: Figuring Gender and Class in Renaissance Literature* (Ithaca: Cornell University Press, 1994).

ing" or "sensing" the truth under a false exterior: "Robes and furred gowns hide all" (4.6.159). Lear seeks to find the earnest "man" under the deceitful decorum — "plate[d] sin with gold." His free-associative screeds are profound moments of guilt and accusation, mostly aimed at reiterating this theme of transcending affected speech. "They flattered me like a dog ....Go to, they are not men o' their words! They told me I was everything," he explains, a brief moment of lucidity, "'Tis a lie, I am not ague-proof" (4.6.94–103). In his very first rambling on the heath, the famous "more sinned against than sinning" speech, we can hear in the "double sense" of his madness this preoccupation with language hiding even his own self-awareness. Speaking to Kent and the Fool, Lear calls for the heavens to find out the truly evil on earth. In one of many invocations to the gods to enforce justice, Lear calls out for discovery and punishment. Once shorn of their exterior veil, criminals will be called to dreadful account. Halfway through this frantic speech, Lear appears to consider himself among the "perjured" now asking for the storm's absolution. Bareheaded and exposed, Lear is asking for the rain to free him from "concealing continents," the ornament of stylized speech itself:

> Let the great gods
> That keep this dreadful pother o'er our heads,
> Find out their enemies now. Tremble, thou wretch,
> That hast within thee undivulged crimes,
> Unwhipped of justice. Hide thee, thou bloody hand;
> Thou perjured, and thou similar of virtue
> That are incestuous. Caitiff, to pieces shake,
> That under covert and convenient seeming
> Has practiced on man's life. Close pent-up guilts
> Rive your concealing continents, and cry
> These dreadful summoners grace. (3.2.48–57)

Shakespeare elaborates on the use of language free from an in-hibiting mode of social address in the character of Kent.[21] Kent is an extension of the play's analysis of flattery, a loose symbol for honest speech, and a foil to Goneril and Regan's manipula-tion of language to acquire elevated social status. Shakespeare teases out of the generic character of the bragging soldier (*miles gloriosus*) one aspect of the idea of remaining steadfast in the face of social decorum, becoming something of a proto-mod-ern symbol of non-conformity. Like Coriolanus, and Hotspur from *Henry IV Part 1*, Kent is incapable of accommodating civil discourse in the new court, which places more emphasis on di-plomacy (represented as effete or emasculating) than martial arts. Kent's reflection on his inability to affect the proper style of address is meant to amplify the play's skepticism of rhetorical deceit. Kent's anger at Oswald (compare Hotspur's anger at the popinjay in *Henry IV Part I*[22]) is one of the funniest in the play and becomes a focal point for the play's hostility toward flattery. Kent's anger also demonstrates a buried class *ressentiment* that functions to ameliorate the deeper anxieties associated with in-strumentalizing rhetoric in the court. Though expressed in the libidinal idiom of Elizabethan jest books — "A knave; a rascal, an eater of broken meats; a base ... three-suited, hundred pound, filthy, worsted stocking knave" (2.2.12–14) — Kent's comic jabs at Oswald provide a window into the curious class politics of the play's critique of flattery as a false vestment. Oswald's "nature" is monstrous because it is the sum of courtly affects tied to linguis-tic accommodation: "You cowardly rascal," Kent says to Oswald, "nature disclaims in thee; a tailor made thee" (2.2.47–48). Corn-wall asks the important question.

CORNWALL: Why art thou angry?

---

21 See Richard Strier's analysis of Kent's anger ("Anger is a privilege," Kent says) in its engagement with Senecan Stoicism in *Unrepentant Renaissance: From Petrarch to Shakespeare to Milton* (Chicago: University of Chicago Press, 2011), 48–53. Madness is the price the play sets to obtain wisdom.
22 William Shakespeare, *Henry IV Part I*, in *The Norton Shakespeare: Based on the Oxford Edition*, 2nd edn. (London: Norton, 2008), 1.3.28–65.

> KENT: That such a slave as this should wear a sword,
> Who wears no honesty. Such smiling rogues as these,
> Like rats, oft bite the holy cords a-twain
> Which are too intrinse t' unloose; smooth every passion
> That in the natures of their lords rebel;
> Bring oil to fire, snow to their colder moods;
> Renege, affirm, and turn their halcyon beaks
> With every gale and vary of their masters,
> Knowing nought, like dogs, but following.
> A plague upon your epileptic visage!
> Smile you my speeches, as I were a fool?
> Goose, if I had you upon Sarum plain,
> I'ld drive ye cackling home to Camelot. (2.2.63–76)

This passage conjures a scene of humanist literacy as too lenient or too accommodating to princely power. Oswald is not just a messenger, he's an advisor (Kent sees him as something of a Polonius). Kent exposes the politics of humanist counsel in the court. The job of humanist council, as Kent screams at Oswald — "superserviceable…bawd to service!" — is to wrap any of the prince's edicts in the shroud of authenticity through legal and historical precedent. Here, reneging and affirming every gale of his masters, Oswald is doing what the humanist project defined as its primary function, offering advice to justices and peers. Kent's response can be compared to the character Hythloday in Thomas More's *Utopia,* who complains about the counselors of kings who "endorse and flatter the most absurd statements of the prince's special favorites, through whose influence they hope to stand well with in the prince."[23] Verifying the prince's strategies of state, the humanist practice of accommodating the court's decrees by offering classical precedent and authority seems shallow, obsequious. Oswald "wears no honesty" in offering false counsel to his master: his duty to his lord, then, appears like an epileptic disease that corrupts power by

---

23 Thomas More, *Utopia,* ed. George Logan and Robert Adams (Cambridge: Cambridge University Press, 1975), 14.

merely justifying the arbitrary whim of royalty. The image is of rats eating through the "holy cords" of real alliances and dynastic bonds. But the contradictions of humanist education are here writ large. We are meant to see Oswald as a kinder, gentler Edmund, a class-climber, he's just following orders, "dutiful" in the same way Kent is, but he's in the unfortunate situation of being on the wrong side of the play's moral fence. His use of courtly display is now the object of an unspoken fear. It is difficult not to read Oswald as the scapegoat to Kent's very own virtue as a faithful follower. Kent is angry because he sees himself in this worsted-stocking knave (or how he is "vested" as Caius anyway). The play searches for a way to reconcile this contradiction by vindicating Kent's "duty" as markedly more honest and therefore stable and just. But not before Shakespeare raises serious questions about the ethics of rhetorical accommodation. If Oswald's mixed garb is a confusion of fashions, a poorly dressed upstart man, "finical rogue" (2.2.16), he nonetheless symbolizes the arbitrary ethics of patronage in the court.

Shakespeare turns this line of thought inside out in one of the most paradoxical moments of the play, when it is Cornwall, the very symbol of a resolute absolutist, who calls out Kent's honest speech:

CORNWALL: This is some fellow,
Who, having been praised for bluntness, doth affect
A saucy roughness, and constrains the garb
Quite from his nature: he cannot flatter, he,
An honest mind and plain, he must speak truth!
An they will take it, so; if not, he's plain.
These kind of knaves I know, which in this plainness
Harbour more craft and more corrupter ends
Than twenty silly ducking observants
That stretch their duties nicely. (2.2.88–99)

Cornwall's complaint about silly court followers is arresting (readers might whisper under their breath the proverb "only Nixon could go to China"), an ethically questionable Duke arguing that honest counsel is a ruse. Cornwall misreads Kent's honesty, but he provides something of a literal reading to Kent's real disguise as Caius. In the scene above, the anagogic resides under the surface of the dialogue. That Kent has to disguise himself in order to remain an "honest" follower is just one example of the play's mystical truths that speak enigmatically through paradoxical images of sacrificial divestment: not only must Kent be false to remain true to his King, but Edgar must experience poverty to keep his estate, Gloucester must lose his eyes to see his condition, Cordelia must become a wife to remain a true daughter … one could add that the Fool must disappear before we really hear him. Cornwall returns to the hermeneutic of reading the hidden self under a constrained garb. His argument that Kent is "affecting" a saucy roughness is, ironically, literally correct insofar as Caius is a performance of the honest soldier. Kent's response is meant to highlight what he finds wrong with Oswald's toady behavior, but his act confirms Cornwall's initial charge of "craft":

> KENT: Sir, in good sooth, in sincere verity,
> Under the allowance of your great aspect,
> Whose influence, like the wreath of radiant fire
> On flickering Phoebus' front, —
> CORNWALL: What mean'st by this? (2.2.96–100)

In his defense, Kent says he "goes out of his dialect" to speak more like the dishonest flatterers of the court who address their masters "in sincere verity," but perhaps Shakespeare has already sown seeds of doubt about who are the silly ducking observants and who the obedient followers.

Proverbs offer an illusory escape from the contradictions of this particular form of scripted identity working to assert place either with or against sovereign will. The tragedy attempts to find another level of remove free from the gravitational force of this economy of rhetoric as intentional performance. Rhetorical vestment is born from the alliance politics of the court, but the alternative to this image of dissembling is not altogether an idealized romantic view of speaking free from social accommodation. The proverbial reflex of speaking through the collective experience provides a different image of scripted speech that is anchored outside these contradictions of vested rhetoric.

Proverbs as Affective Tools

> No rescue? What, a prisoner?…
> No seconds? All myself?
> Why, this would make a man a man of salt,
> To use his eyes for garden water-pots,
> Aye, and laying autumn's dust.
> — *King Lear* 4.6.184–91

Following Burke's idea of proverbs offering strategies for survival, I want to move the discussion from the rhetorical vestment to scripted adage, from doublespeak as mask to rehearsed locution as coping mechanism. The difference between these two sentiments is cutting proverbial hairs, perhaps, but a good way to frame the difference might be to think of modern philosophical correlates. Martin Heidegger's attitude toward "the they" (*das Man*) might serve as an interesting analogy. According to Graham Harman, Heidegger's project — the definition of *Dasein* — centered on removing oneself from the controlling forces of modern "fallen" existence, a modernist sentiment over the homogenizing forms of industrial life that conforms to norms of a mass culture, accommodating to standards of habituated life. Heidegger's various triadic solutions reinforce the complex we've been considering, a "return" to the *Volk* wisdom offered in his analogies of ur-tools — hammers, built huts in the Black Forest, and advice to "choose a hero" and repeat the patterns of behavior to free oneself from a somnambulant "ready to hand" proverbial tool world. To free oneself from the automatic life by, ironically, adapting to and performing the repetition of deeply-rooted emblematic acts.[24] I will return to Heidegger in the final chapter to flesh out these theoretical tangents, but for now I want to point to the similarities between the problem and solution to Heidegger's project. We are in a position to see the performance of proverbial speech as one element of the tragedy's deeper solution on mnemonic modes of expression. Considering those enlightened moments when Lear is witness to social injustice, it is hard not to read the king's belated awareness of pharisaical fraud as a screed against hypocrisy in all its forms, a political awareness of corruption that comes too little and too late: "The usurer hangs the cozener....Robes and furred gowns hide all" (4.6.157–58). His imagined solution to this problem, said to an already blind Gloucester on the heath, is to "Get thee glass eyes; / And, like a scurvy Politian, seem / To see the things thou dost not" (4.6.164–66). *Seem* to see. These words are meant to describe the way wealthy magnates and justices turn their back on corruption and the mistreatment of the poor. But Lear's prescription of glass eyes also hints at another analogy important to our turn from looking at discourse as alienation or sustenance. I would urge that this moment of political enlightenment in the play (arguably Lear's epiphany about political reality) is charged with a special meaning today in the way it characterizes the moment of self-reflection implicit in any materialist "critique," the demystification of literary representation as ideology. Post-Marxist analysis of false consciousness can speak from a rationalist position that posits a view of the real as objective, relatively neutral or "free" from the logic of the system it analyzes.[25] The glass eyeballs are an image of objective "discernment" — Althusser's promise of a science that maps theories of the real from a "relative autonomy" — but they are also a symbol of an uncanny if not disturbing indifference to the world. Physical disfigurement and seeming care for a world that

---

24 Graham Harman, *Heidegger Explained: From Phenomenon to Thing.* (Peru, IL: Open Court, 2007), 55–78.

25 See Philip Goldstein, "Althusserian Theory: From Scientific Truth to Institutional History," special issue on "The Legacy of Althusser," *Studies in Twentieth-Century Literature* 18.1 (1994): 14–26.

finally advances the project of modernity is not the solution that will lead us from the heath. Can we read this as a challenge to return to some of the proverbial sentiment in the play, and this in spite of the prosthetic stoicism that offers little hope?

Throughout *King Lear*, Shakespeare depicts characters speaking "in script," as if these characters return to an earlier form of literacy associated with childhood learning: imitation, the recursive pedagogy that emphasized mimicry and mnemonic forms of stylized speech, with its emphasis on patterning intelligence through the habit of repetition. No less an image of automata, we are asked to question how speaking in this blank voice is not also an ersatz performance of artificially contrived affective postures to the world. The prevalence of proverbial speech in the play has been noted before by other literary scholars who see the adage as a thematic framing device and less a reflection of older literacy practices or posthuman pathology. Richard Harp's analysis describes the quantity of proverbs: "Lear utters more proverbs than anyone else in the play — forty-eight by my count — followed by the Fool with thirty-five (making him relatively the most proverbial of all the characters) and Edgar with nineteen."[26] Dent counts 176 proverbs total in the play.[27] How many proverbs are used is probably not the point, but when and why certainly does matter. On this, Harp avers: "These proverbs are often spoken in times of stress: Lear on the heath, the Fool being the Fool, Edgar disguised as Poor Tom, and Kent, also in disguise and making use of maxims in his contentious exchanges with Oswald and Cornwall."[28] Harp does not count the coining of proverbial speech, but he does notice what he calls "compressed speech" and "pointed phrasing sum[ming] up sharply an important part of the play's overall wisdom" working in scenes throughout.[29] The tragic arc of the play means

26 Richard Harp, "Proverbs and Philosophy in *The Merchant of Venice* and *King Lear*," *Ben Jonson Journal* 16 (1995): 211 [197–215].

27 R.W. Dent, *Shakespeare's Proverbial Language: An Index* (Berkeley: University of California Press, 1981).

28 Harp, "Proverbs and Philosophy," 211.

29 Ibid.

that most of the citational proverbs occur near the end, as characters face violence and destruction. Shakespeare intuits what modern psychology terms "perseveration," where individuals respond to trauma by repeating words or phrases that seem to lack an appropriate stimulus. The current medical description of this disorder — a "form of involuntary recall resulting from uncontrolled postactivation of normally inhibited memory traces" — could be used to explain Lear's seemingly unprovoked "thought insertions" and regression to primal scenes of betrayal.[30] If the play begins staging the problem of rehearsed speech, it ends with scenes of characters speaking through recollected language. Moreover, frequency of proverbial insertions in the end of the play parallels Lear's return to a state of childhood dependency. What we hear in many of these hollow proclamations in *Lear* are characters pulling back from the present within their proverbial insertions, seeking refuge in the palliative effects of familiar speech. We sense in these terse lines throughout *Lear* a return to preconceived rituals of habituated thought, the return to adage and proverb, phrases that have been previously written in some collective tablet of memory. In the remainder of the chapter I want to look more closely at how the logic of this process works by looking at scenes where aphoristic reflection helps characters record and make sense of the conflict and destruction around them. There are several moments in the play that show us characters wavering from the stark image of violence and cruelty by receding into the commonplace adage. How to account for *King Lear*'s aesthetic rendering of tragic loss, this form of accounting for the world's destruction that allows a re-

---

30 Patrick McNamara and Martin Albert write, "[P]erseveration is essentially a failure of inhibition of normally inhibited memory traces or a failure to resist interference from activation of these normally inhibited memory traces. It is possible that unsuccessful attempts to access a target from the lexicon may trigger the activation of previous targets that have been strongly primed and have escaped suppression because of inhibition." "Neuropharmacology of Verbal Perseveration," *Seminars in Speech and Language* 25.4 (2004): 309–21, http://www.bu.edu/lab/files/2011/03/McNamara_Albert_2004.pdf.

cuperative reaction to the stark face of violence by re-*meming* it through the familiar?

Use of the proverb at the beginning of the play still belongs partly to the world of dissembling. But these earlier scenes stage how the adage works to write self-reflection, how the blank voice is inscribed by affective response. If common-placed wisdom is the ideological life-blood of self-display in the court, it does not surprise us to see the first appearance of this form of address in the beginning of the play in an exchange between Goneril and Regan. Right after we have witnessed the spectacle of Goneril and Regan's use of flattery, we see both of them meet to discuss their father. Regan explains, "'Tis the infirmity of his age; yet he hath ever but slenderly known himself." And in response Goneril replies: "The best and soundest of his time hath been but rash" (1.1.293). Where does this sentiment come from? Who is speaking? The line is a perfect example of this aphoristic recording, as it seems to come from a scripted, mnemonic self who delivers the lines from a vantage point of rational calculation. The line exists before it is articulated, and we sense that it has been inscribed in a table of memory under the category of "Being Rash." Goneril does this again, later, when speaking with Oswald about her father's infirm condition, "Old fools are babes again, and must be used / With checks as flatteries, when they are abused" (1.3.19–20). An oddly reflexive line, for Goneril, as we hear her echoing a line from memory that allows her to frame her earlier dissembling as a waste of time when dealing with Lear's ingratitude. Albany upbraids his wife Goneril for her treatment of Lear, saying, "you are not worth the dust which the rude wind / Blows in your face" (4.2.31–32). He chastises her about the "material sap" of a tree that "must wither / and come to deadly use." (4.2.36–37). "No more, the text is foolish," Goneril explains, acknowledging the catechism for what it is. Albany's response is telling, since it seems coded to speak to the person most engaged in the use of aphorism as a strategy of rhetorical legerdemain. "Wisdom and goodness to the vile seem vile; / Filths savor but themselves" (4.2.39–40). Albany's response can be read as an attempt to speak the devil's own language: I will offer a proverb about the blindness of the wicked in a tongue it will understand.

Cordelia's notorious complaint after the initial love test sets the frame for this "contest" of proverbial speech. She is complaining that her sisters' "true" selves are missing from these moments of articulation, but we might reflect on the oddly inert quality of a speech act whose "purpose" or intention seems to reside in a book that lurks behind the voice. Shakespeare intuits, I think, the scripted quality of this self in some of his own figurative language: Cordelia tells her father "it is no vicious blot, murder, or foulness … That deprived me of your grace," equating the act of blotting a line of writing with a crime (1.1.225–27). And France's rejoinder, explaining "a tardiness in nature / Which often leaves the history unspoken / That it intends to do," imagines identity prewritten in some history that exists before its reading, its utterance foretold in a kind of memory book of historical unfolding (1.1.237–39). These meta-moments are even more disturbing because they articulate the problem of locating identity in a manner that is itself indicative of the aphoristic style. The rote use of commemorative speech, in this instance, is not so much functioning to mark an identity as it is to preserve it through a kind of animatronic speech.

When Goneril and Regan "disquantify" Lear's "train" of followers, the lines seem to hover around the idea of old age affecting wisdom as proffered in the Bible: Goneril explains: "As you are old and reverend, you should be wise" (1.4.215). This line echoes Proverbs 19:20 from the King James Bible: "Hear counsel, and receive instruction, that thou mayest be wise in thy latter end." Lear has made it to old age, but the audience is asked to question the sincerity of the advice as another instance of hypocrisy, the devil citing scripture. Goneril's appropriation of biblical authority provides a modicum of license to assert her dominance over her father: the stereotype of aged wisdom reciting proverbial advice to youth is treated to carnival inversion. Later, Regan echoes Goneril's proverbial wisdom in an earnest key:

O, sire, you are old;
Nature in you stands on the very verge
Of her confine. You should be ruled and led
By some discretion, that discerns your state
Better than you yourself. Therefore, I pray you,
That to our sister you do make return;
Say you have wronged her, sir. (2.4.139–44)

Regan twists this adage from Proverbs 2:1, "Discretion shall preserve thee, understanding shall keep thee." Lear is meant to hear
the subtle instruction to "please understand." But this cinches
it for Lear, who will not sit patiently and be told to confess.
Lear is incapable of valuing filial gratitude from anything but
the crudest of materialist terms: "I'll go with thee," he says to
Goneril about her offer to keep fifty of his one hundred followers, "Thy fifty yet doth double five-and-twenty. / And thou art
twice her love" (2.4.253–54). Regan's proverb is used as a tool to
unseat Lear's authority, proving true the Fool's earlier prophetic
description of Lear: "[T]hou madest thy daughter thy mother:
for when thou gavest them the rod, and put'st down thine own
breeches" (1.4.150). Goneril and Regan have assumed the position as schoolmaster lecturing Lear through the adage. The instruction reproduces the sentiment of Erasmus's many citations
of common experience providing practical wisdom to the Fool:
experience is the schoolhouse of fools. Erasmus comes back to
the idea of punitive experience time and again: "only pain instructs the fool."[31] There is a clever turning in on the scene of
literacy in these initial uses of proverbial speech. Regan's defense
of her treatment of her father is a familiar enough reprise: "O,
sir, to willful men, / The injuries that they themselves procure /
Must be their schoolmasters" (3.1.297–99).

   If Goneril and Regan are banishing Lear from their domestic
care, they are doing so as schoolmasters offering catechism on
the virtues of learning one's place. Regan and Goneril appropriate proverbial speech in ways that conform to early modern

31   Erasmus, *Adages,* 33.

attitudes about rote learning. Repeating maxims is meant to pattern the unconscious mind, to create the "grain" of the inward
thought, as Vives pictured *copia* being magically inscribed onto
the private page of the student's imagination, "meete for familiar
speech ... when tyme requyreth."[32] It is no surprise then when
Lear, early on, seems to speak to himself through the same language used by his daughters. In the very first moment of experiencing resistance to his authority from Cornwall, we hear him
pause and retreat to this space:

> My breath and blood!
> Fiery? The fiery duke? Tell the hot duke that —
> No, but not yet. May be he is not well.
> Infirmity doth still neglect all office.
> Whereto our health is bound; we are not ourselves
> When nature, being oppressed, commands the mind
> To suffer with the body. (2.4.98–103)

Imagining Cornwall as ill, Lear cautions himself not to go mad.
But he is really speaking about himself: "we are not ourselves
when ...." He retreats to an inward space to echo a proverbial
sentiment about infirmity, speaking through the proffered wisdom offered by his daughters earlier. The collective voice of the
adage ties Lear to Cornwall (or so he imagines), and the al-
tered voice occasions a communal sense of patience for Lear.
The coining of proverbial wisdom offers an affective response of
calm from Lear's normally impetuous assertions. Lear's performance of the citational adage also rationalizes his limits within
his environment, where "all [the] office" of his duty to proper
modes of address is subject to the health and well being of his
body. Oddly vacant yet palliative, the retreat to the blank voice

---

32 Juan Luis Vives, "Of the Mind," in *Introduction to Wisdom, trans. Sir Richard Moryson, 1540.* Quoted in *Vives: On Education: A Translation of the De
Tradendis Disciplinis of Juan Luis Vives,* ed. and trans. Foster Watson (Cambridge: Cambridge University Press, 1913), xxxix.

allows Lear a brief cessation of contentions from court and status.

However the idea that his physical state has weakened his reason is precisely the idea that his daughters seize upon to foster Lear's compliance to their domestic rule. Regan instructs him: "Nature in you stands on the very verge / Of her confine. You should be ruled and led / By some discretion" (2.4.139–41). The Fool is quick to note this. His language points to the stock image of inverted domestic order to remind Lear he has not maintained the upper hand. The scene is where Gloucester is sent to get Regan after seeing Kent in the stocks. Lear is about to lose his patience:

> LEAR: O me, my heart, my rising heart! But, down!
> FOOL: Cry to it, nuncle, as the cockney did to the eels when she put 'em in the paste alive; she knapped 'em o' the coxcombs with a stick, and cried "Down, wantons, down!" 'Twas her brother that, in kindness to his horse, buttered his hay. (2.4.115–18)

The Fool has made Lear's "heart" one of the eels in this comic language. He is telling Lear that his soft-hearted treatment of his daughters is as foolish as the housewife who will not kill the eels before baking them in a pie (and, moreover, her husband's a fool because he butters his horse's hay). Eels appear in a few English proverbs: whipping eels, beating them down by the "coxcomb" (who is beating whom?). A woman beating a man can also allude directly to Lear's treatment: he's beaten down in the image. The image of the eel seems rustic and appropriately *non sequitur,* coming from the Fool, but buried in the reference to the eel is a coded commentary on Regan and Goneril's stratagem to control Lear's self-image. The popular age-old adage "to hunt eels" was used to refer to the practice of stirring the bottom of the river to lift eels from the surface in order to harvest them. As an adage, it was used by scholars to describe the Machiavellian practice of benefiting from your enemy's misfortune, to "stir the pot" in order to take advantage of confusion. Erasmus explains:

> The metaphor arises from the fact that those who hunt eels catch nothing if the water remains still, only when they stir the water up and down and thoroughly muddy it do they catch them ....This art, alas, is understood only too well by certain princes who because of their desire for power sow discord between states or stir up war on some pretext so that they can freely tax the wretched common people and satisfy their greed by starving absolutely innocent citizens.[33]

The Fool's allusion to the proverbial eel is a warning to Lear. He is offering a prescriptive image of political inversion of domestic space. But he is also hinting at the King's precarious mental situation as the object of Regan and Goneril's strategy to capitalize on his distraction.

In the first part of the play, then, proverbial language still orbits around the idea of rhetorical deceit. But it shows us how the inward space of proverbial reflection is patterned from social contest: Goneril and Regan's provisional use of the adage gets inside Lear and has its due effect. Moreover, the Fool's path to Lear's madness, as it were, is to speak proverbially to his inward condition. The staging of proverbial effect begins to fade when Regan puts Lear's trust in their counsel to the test. Regan explains to Lear that she is really not ready for his visit (odd, given she speaks this as a guest of Gloucester's manor): "I looked not for you yet, nor am provided / For your fit welcome." She adds that he must go back to Goneril, "Give ear, sir, to my sister" (2.4.226–27). And she rounds it with proverbial sagacity: "For those that mingle reason with your passion / Must be content to think you old" (2.4.228–29). Regan not only affects the wisdom of the schoolmaster, but suggests that Lear's angry curses need an interpreter: his passion will need footnotes for people to understand him at all. Not too far from the truth, this, or at least it is prophetic of Lear's later erratic protestations on the heath. Lear's response is telling: "Is this well-spoken?" (2.4.232). He means to say, "are you addressing me with the right degree

33 Erasmus, *Adages*, 279.

of respect?" But he also suggests that the game is over, in a way, pulling the mask off the use of adage to affect distance, authority and false camaraderie. The entire trick of affecting proverbial speech to assert status is exposed as a sport of linguistic modulation.

The Art of Necessities: Animatronic Speech as Panacea

> When the mind's free,
> The body's delicate.
> — *King Lear* 3.4.12–13

From here on the use of adage takes a turn, as it is no longer articulated from the cynical perspective and exposed as a strategy for imparting false wisdom to control another. As we briefly discussed above, Lear's experience on the heath reproduces one of Erasmus's main proverbial sentiments in his major writings: "Experience is the best teacher." "Trouble experienced makes a fool wise." His allegorical character Folly, notorious for speaking in adage, comes back to this theme almost as a recursive tic. "One simple design" of *Praise of Folly,* observes Clarence Miller, "is the sixfold repetition of the proverbial tag *taedium vitae,* which highlights one of Folly's poses and one of her major arguments: with world-weary resignation she insists folly can sweeten man's unalterably bitter lot and render it bearable."[34] In his *Adagiorum,* Erasmus places Hesiod's proverb in prominence: "His punishment the wicked man receives / At last, but only pain instructs the fool."[35] One could easily see Lear's trial in the storm as a postscript playing out the enigmatical vision of this dominant proverbial tenet. When the Fool speaks to Lear in Act 2, he continues to perform proverbs as cautionary tools that come with implied affective postures. "O nuncle," the Fool tells Lear as

---

34 Clarence Miller, "The Logic and Rhetoric of Proverbs in Erasmus' Praise of Folly," in *Humanism and Style: Essay on Erasmus and More,* ed. Clarence Miller and Jerry Harp (Bethlehem: Lehigh University Press, 2011), 56.

35 Erasmus, *Adages,* 33.

he bristles against the wind and the prospects of being homeless on the heath, "court holy-water in a dry house is better than this rain-water out o'door" (3.2.10). This is a reference to the age-old proverb of selling favor in the court by exploiting one's proximity to the prince. Erasmus mentions it in the context of "selling smoke," or, to sell the favor of the great.

> There is a proverbial saying bandied about in our own time regarding the splendid promises of courtiers. For they talk of 'court incense,' thinking of that incense-vapor which is wafted in our sacred rites from a swinging censer....They speak too of the 'holy water' of courtiers, thinking of the water which is placed at the door of churches, for those to sprinkle themselves with who go in or come out.[36]

The Fool is helping Lear consider his decision to brace against the elements over acquiescing to Goneril and Regan's authority, accepting the dubious ethics of the court rather than struggling to make it through the night. The proverbial sentiment reminds the audience of the glib and oily politics of dissembling, but measures this environment in crudely ecological terms: compromise ethics or health?

Throughout the scene on the heath, Shakespeare reflects on the power of proverbial language to sustain us when facing nature's indifference to human need. "The art of our necessities is strange, / That can make vile things precious" (3.2.68–69), Lear says in a moment of hesitation before stepping into the hovel. Lear's line appears as a thought insertion, as if speaking to himself, reminding himself of an adage to gauge his affective position to the "unkind elements" before him. This is an eerily blank voice that seems to come to us from the echo of mnemonic reflection patterned by proverbial inscription. The adage speaks to human adaptation and the way environmental stresses have a value free from human economies of status. Lear's citational phrasing performs the magic of turning nature's indif-

36   Ibid., 69.

ference to a positive value, a lesson in elemental continuance. This proverbial insight closely echoes the idea of Diomedian necessity — that some conditions force us to act in unexpected ways — but proffers an understanding of surmounting physical stress through the repetition of learned responses. That is, by "accounting" for the uncanny indifference of a cold world, by recognizing it, and naming it, through the adage, Lear endures. The adage makes vile things precious.

Edgar's lines on the heath, while in character as Poor Tom, echo proverbial sentiment. His use of proverb in the play emphasizes the citational quality of adage as characters experience violence and neglect:

When we our betters see bearing our woes,
We scarcely think our miseries our foes.
Who alone suffers suffers most i' the mind,
Leaving free things and happy shows behind:
But then the mind much sufferance doth o'er skip,
When grief hath mates, and bearing fellowship.
How light and portable my pain seems now,
When that which makes me bend makes the king bow.
(3.6.95–108)

Edgar's soliloquy reiterates the time-honored adage "misery loves company," but its couplets instantiate a new citational turn in the play, as many of the proverbial expressions from this point onward mark out this palliative reflection. The sentiment that "the mind much sufferance doth o'er skip, / When grief hath mates" could be said to foreground the communal salve of the proverbial voice. When characters stop a scene to insert such common saws, they are not alone but share a collective experience that assuages the annihilating power of their solitary grief. "How light and portable my pain seems now," he finishes.

In one of the most grisly scenes of all in Shakespeare, Gloucester screams "He that will think to live till he be old, / Give me some help!" (3.7.70–71). The adage "to love to live, and live to love" haunts the cadence of Gloucester's scream for help, as if the call to adage flashes before his eyes too late. The audience cannot help but feel the irony of the moment, as the Christian sentiment underscores such a violent desecration of Gloucester's provenance of manor-house ethics as he is accused and attacked by those who received his grace. There are moments when this hollow mechanical voice signifies an oddly vacant self buried in the adage, reeling in horror, a voice that is less than rational, nearly unconscious. Listen to Gloucester's proverbial inscription on the heath in the next scene: "Our means secure us, and our mere defects / Prove our commodities" (4.1.21–22).

Gloucester's assertion is meant to rationalize his fate, but it appears unmotivated in this instance — "uncontrolled postactivation" — as if visited by a fading thought. The proverbial voice functions to turn distress into a delayed lesson, its magic is to turn lack and privation into a stoic lesson about finding strength in one's "defects." But the quality of the perfunctory "scripted" tone is tinged with the sense of an involuntary, synthetic incantation. As we have seen, Edgar earlier uses this tone when he muses, alone on stage, watching Kent, the Fool, and the blind Gloucester lead Lear to Dover: "When we our betters see bearing our woes, / We scarcely think our miseries our foes … " (3.6.95–96). Like Goucester's "postactivated" assertion, these lines are less a spontaneous reflection on one's plight, and more like a mechanical recitation. It is peculiar that the inward landscape of trauma is described as free only when it leaves behind a pretended "show." Edgar is thinking about how he cannot share the misery of watching his father's plight without giving himself away, but the line could stand as a marker of the new tone the play takes against mnemonic speech. Yet this moment of intense privacy is rendered in a maxim that vaguely reflects the scripted forms of memory work we have discussed as humanist literacy.

How can we account for the use of this singsong parsing in self-reflection? Edgar is, effectively, alone on stage to work through a programmed response to the violence erupting around him, an early modern moment of posthuman "processing" through files that have encoded habits of mind scribbled out beforehand. Edgar is framing the vision of the forced inversion of authority and order on the heath and he speaks as if from a book of moral solace. Shakespeare is depicting the memory work involved in trying to see the traumatic present through a language that would render it intelligible. Where does the subject retreat, he seems to ask, when under duress but back to a previously learned adage that renders the destruction knowable.

Much has been said about the providential discourse that writes some of the characters of the play. Edgar, Albany, and Gloucester, in particular, express faith in a divine justice (and, by implication, the ethos of Christian patience) that can intimate the worst atrocity as a sign of a future reckoning. The most compelling scenes in the play are when these "providentialists" reach to rationalize the social discord as a sign of impending apocalypse:

GLOUCESTER: Tis the time's plague, when madmen lead the blind. (4.1.48)

EDGAR: Men must endure.
Their going hence, even as their coming hither. (5.2.9–10)

"That I am wretched," the blind Gloucester tells his son Edgar, disguised as a vagabond "makes thee happier. Heavens, deal so still" (4.1.65–66). Such lines explain the present violence and economic dearth as a sign of providential accounting, figuring the pain of physical suffering as an unfulfilled moment of divine justice. Any form of suffering is merely the sign of a future redemptive justice. The hopeful proclamations in the play orbit around the play's otherwise skeptical treatment of suffering, a deeply psychological process of symbolic compensation: "This shows you are above, / You justicers, that these our nether crimes / So speedily can venge!" (4.2.79–81). What we feel when sensing the inert quality of these rote responses to the social and political destruction depicted in the play is what I call animatronic speech, an eerily dispassionate memorized phrase that is recited like a chant. If the articulation of providential thought seems oddly disconnected from the moments of social discord, perhaps it is less Shakespeare's use of skepticism to distance us from the real, than it is an attempt to find a way to preserve a moment in memory in proverbial form, to twine Benjamin's own proverbial moral around the ivy wall.

As we discussed above, Jameson tries to recover the regenerative impulse, describing the proverb as a technique whose strategy is to "carve with clean large strokes" an image of somatic recognition lived in the very structure of the language, where "the temporal sequence remains absorbed in the syntax of the sentence."[37] When considering one example of Brecht's use of proverb, we see how the trope comes to life to reinforce the playwright's political project. The poem is from *The Caucasian Chalk Circle*:

> When a great man's house collapses
> Many little people get crushed
> Those with no share in the mighty's fortune
> Often share their fate. The wagon's downfall
> Tugs the sweating oxen with it
> Into the abyss.[38]

Jameson considers how a simple poem has such authority because we find ourselves "confronted with the mysteries of the definite article ....These particular oxen have no previous history, no farm to describe, no family ownership or paths to market, precisely because they are not 'particular' oxen at all."[39] Jameson continues to explain how the effect of using such placeless articles is equivalent to that of reification itself:

> I think we must look behind these ostensible characters, these extras and supernumeraries of the scene — who are its protagonists by virtue of the very fact they are supernumeraries — to the thought mode which sees them as such,

37 Jameson, *Brecht and Method,* 136.
38 Ibid.
39 Ibid.

and identifies them in its great flat homogenous categories. For as has already been observed, these syntactical items have been crystallized and reified into the token of an experience everybody knows and recognizes in advance, in a tacit collective experience that need not be explained. The definite article therefore presupposes a kind of peasant history — that is to say, the paradoxically changeless and immemorial, stagnant history, which is not yet history in our modern sense.[40]

Jameson wants to argue that Brecht's use of proverbs is consistent with his alienation effect in that the modern playwright uses them to reinforce his lessons on life under capitalism, what he calls a "homeopathic method in which reification is used to dereify and to bring change and new momentum to customary behavior and stereotypical 'values.'"[41] He admits that this particular use of proverbs, then, "seems inconsistent with any initially 'biblical' or proverbial style principle, which sought to create familiar and reified entities by way of the definite article."[42] Nonetheless, Jameson advances a useful set of terms by which we may define the proverb as a moment of speech that functions as an early modern equivalent of the "bullet time" of Hollywood's ultra-slow motion sequences that organize, for the spectator's eye, objects free from time and gravity. These objects are bracketed from Kantian absolutes in this way, allowing the audience to ponder their place in a static unfolding. In the moment before things resume their anticipated life of cause and effect, the world is "crystallized" in a "collective experience that need not be explained."[43]

How is the objective, rational tone of animatronic speech different from the "glass eyes" suggested above, in Lear's metaphor for the hypocrisy of social indifference and political quietude?

40 Ibid., 136–37.
41 Ibid., 133.
42 Ibid.
43 Ibid., 137.

Shakespeare's "two-eyed" aesthetic rendering of human automata sets this view of scripted speech in contrast to the animalistic imagery throughout the play. On one hand, the image of "speaking and purposing not" to deceive others, can be read as a further elaboration on duplicity: falsehood is coterminous with hidden "centaurs" (4.6.121), "gilded serpents" (5.3.85), greedy "wolves" (3.4.87), "sea monsters" (1.4.238), "detested kites" (1.4.239). Ironically, this bestiary of monstrous guile defines the civilized world of humanist rhetoric and stylized modes of competitive address as predacious. Which is more human? Rhetoric in the court, or mnemonic speech on the heath? The inhuman and fragmentary speech of habitual proverbs seems to trouble the species-boundary that defines human exceptionalism. It is the autonomic heath that is posed as an antithetical escape from this world, a defensive retreat that allows for continuance and survival. The human penchant for mnemonic language promises a different "reversion" in terms of human evolutionary history, as it were, as the play provides an image of characters returning to an imagined collective experience of ritualized behavior.

As I discussed above, Dollimore's famous reading of the last lines can figure as a test case for "critique," as he sees tragedy's power akin to the Brechtian affect of demystifying conventional thought. I wonder if Dollimore's clever reading isn't symptomatic of literary criticism's dream of escaping the gravity of the play's pessimism by revising it as social critique or philosophical musing. This has been argued before, but my point is that the move to contextualize the ending as ironic is itself a kind of analgesic retreat, its own way of turning our back on the severe nihilism of the play. A way to follow Kent, not to death (I see his "journey" to "follow" his master as suicide), but perhaps off the stage. What might it mean to see the expressions of providentialism as moments of animatronic speech? Such an accounting might mean following Edgar's lead, instead, accounting for the "sad time" in a way that measures the weight of the pronouncement, to move forward in a way that preserves knowledge of the powerful loss, to remember the past as if chiseled in stone, but in a way that protects us from our future, life approving the common saw.

CHAPTER THREE

Accessorizing *King Lear* in the Anthropocene

O ruin'd piece of nature! This great world
Shall so wear out to naught.
— *King Lear* 4.6.132–33

Man's life's as cheap as beasts.
— *King Lear* 2.4.262

Aesop himself is said to have been a misshapen hump-
backed slave; his home is transferred to Phrygia, i.e. to
the country where the transition is made from immediate symbolism, and attachment to nature, to the country
in which man begins to apprehend the spiritual and his
own self.
— Hegel, *Lecture on Aesthetics,* part II[1]

Thinking Bare Art

Can we read *King Lear* as its own cautionary marker? If so, what
is it warning us against? Ruined nature? About refusing love? Living in a world without god(s)? But can we really make the narrative speak as a parable without detracting from its significance?
It seems an absurd question, since asking such a thing begs the

1   G.W.F. Hegel, *Aesthetics: Lectures on Fine Art,* part II, ed. Hotho, trans. T.M.
    Knox, 1973, https://www.marxists.org/reference/archive/hegel/works/ae/
    part2.htm.

worst kind of reductionism. To approach the text as simple admonition is to insist on the prescriptive over the reflective, or the practical over the imaginative, to insist on narrative as a tool for communicating practical concerns of the everyday. To force any literary text to speak to utilitarian affairs in this way seems to detract from its aesthetic value. However, following Burke's clever overlay of literature as a kind of proverbial medicine, I would argue it is worth the risk to follow *King Lear*'s nostalgic return in its embrace of lost practices, in this case *imitatio,* the whole system of posturing action through mnemonic prescripts. To think of narrative in such ways is to reclaim for literature its sociological (and I would argue anthropological) function to proffer "matters of welfare," as Burke terms it: "promise, admonition, solace, vengeance, foretelling, instruction."[2] There may be a crippling idealism at work in any anxiety we have about meddling with the sacred art text as removed from the petty affairs of our practical readings. To push back on modern aesthetics means to reclaim the Renaissance ideal of utilizing the works of the past to assert their potential to shape consensus around a practical ethics.

It could be argued that the story of our reluctance to forgo aesthetic idealism is linked to larger myths about civilization and human progress. If we can imagine using *Lear* as a parable of the posthuman, we might begin by tracing this idealization of aesthetics against our posthuman backdrop. Parables, like proverbs, were considered during the Renaissance to be one of the ancient forms of passing down maxims to future generations. But in the modern period, the parable is relegated to a secondary status.[3] Before offering a parable of *Lear,* I want to discuss how the fable tradition is, like its half-cousin the proverb, perceived as a prescriptive poetic form. In his *Aesthetics* (1835), Hegel separated poetry from prose in ways that corresponded

2   Kenneth Burke, *The Philosophy of Literary Form: Studies in Symbolic Action* (New York: Vintage Books, 1941), 296.
3   For a forceful history of the importance of the fable to English Restoration polemics, see Annabel Patterson, *Fables of Power: Aesopian Writing and Political History* (Durham: Duke University Press, 1991).

to his understanding of Western society's evolution toward abstract thought and self-consciousness: human civilization progressed from a base world of practical prose to an advanced world of verse and embodied symbolism. A strange mapping of history, if you think about it, its own fantasy of evolutionary development, where humans move not from hunter–gatherers to farmers, but from didactic realists to organic symbolists. Prose was the "first stage" of artistic representation, associated with manual labor and "the slave," free only of second-order metaphors and symbols that allowed for the advanced conceptual calculus important for civilization. "In the slave, prose begins, and so this entire species is prosaic too."[4]

There is an imperialist fantasy that informs this narrative picture of aesthetic progress, to be certain, but my point is that our fears of flirting with art's aura to assert its practical "use value" is not entirely removed from Hegel's teleology. Hegel imagines a moment in the historical past where the concrete language of proverbs and parables were the practical tools in the struggle with Nature. His hierarchical ordering of genres as "stages" of artistic progress through the ages reads like a manual in the archeology of representation, depicting the human progress through valleys of ancient writing, merely "descriptive prose," fables, parables, and proverbs, to the more fertile plains of advanced symbolic mysticism and, eventually, the sublime. We could think of his romantic privileging of the symbolic over the real, then, as a first-world narrative of its own kind. The privileging of the rich interplay of allegory and anagogic reasoning favored over the sparse didactic representation of tool-being is equivalent to a valuing of animal protein over plant protein, say, where the symbolic depends on the transmission of the real object within the metaphor to begin with for its "consumption," but, like the analogy implies, requires eight times the amount of fuel to make possible its surplus of symbolic meanings. If such a comparison seems forced, consider Hegel's hierarchy of artistic representations, his own language devaluing proverbs, parables,

4   Hegel, *Aesthetics*.

and fables as kinds of lean art that do not stray far enough from what he called the "material" of their representation. Such art belonged, he imagined, to a world of everyday moral advice. Hegel's list of misfit prose genres is really a list of oral traditions: fable, parable, apologue (moral fable), proverb, and metamorphoses (myths of regeneration and change). It is also the world of Aesop and his misshapen body — relegated in its twisted way to the drudge service of didacticism. In these lesser forms of art, then, we find a form of representation doomed to a dependent existence, in service to a master of its "related single situation."[5] In this instance the master is a single idea of a human endeavor whose message, adorned in a riddle or fable, holds sway and never frees itself from the immediate world of necessity. This is the starting point of concrete artistic representation:

> In the first the concrete phenomenon, whether drawn from
> nature or from human affairs, events, and actions, consti-
> tutes the starting-point, but also the important and essential
> thing for the representation. It is selected indeed only on
> account of the more general meaning which it contains
> and alludes to, and it is only so far explained as the aim
> of illustrating this meaning in *a related single situation or
> event demands* ....Works of art which make this form their
> foundation remain therefore of a subordinate kind, and
> their content cannot be the Absolute itself but some *different
> and restricted situation or occurrence; on this account the
> forms belonging here are used in the main only occasionally
> as accessories.*[6]

For Hegel, proverbs and fables are trapped in the immediate sensory world of the here-and-now, mere "accessories" or
tools of literal communication: proverbs and parables "adduce
an individual case which is drawn for the most part from day-
to-day human life, but which is then to be taken in a universal

5   Ibid.
6   Ibid. Emphasis mine.

meaning."[7] But enslaved to its original "day-to-day," the comparisons or analogies implied in the adage never take flight from the didactic message of the representation. "These are not comparisons where the universal meaning and the concrete phenomenon appear outside one another and contrast with one another. The former is immediately expressed with the latter."[8]

Hegel imagines this learned art as coming from a specific place in his archeology of the artistic forms. Implied in his narrative of aesthetic awareness is an unspoken theory of human need driving artistic function, an image of human want motoring the need for specific forms of artistic representation, where bare worlds require bare words, a kind of boiling down to the kernel of narrative form. According to Hegel, this lean art is doomed to its prescriptive function, one that can only speak of consequences and implications, but it also appears trapped outside of the self-identity he imagined in the "higher" artistic representations. Annabel Patterson describes Hegel's view of fables as an aesthetic bias against pragmatism: "What Hegel argued," she avers,

> was the remoteness of a fabulist mode of representation — an arbitrary and explicit comparison between an intended signified and some natural phenomenon — from the unconscious, unpremeditated union between symbol and transcendental signified he required for true art. For Hegel the fabulist deals in mere wit, rather than depth of insight, and he restricts himself to observing such trivialities as animal habits.[9]

Hegel pictures the subject of bare art as one with its material world: his model assumes that life is outside itself, trapped in a world of necessity and practicality. Giorgio Agamben might define this idea of bare art as one that captures or replays the

7   Ibid.
8   Ibid.
9   Patterson, *Fables of Power,* 240–42.

"openness" of an immediate world or environment he describes belonging to animal consciousness.

> For the animal, beings are open but not accessible; that is to say, they are open in an inaccessibility and an opacity .... This openness without disconcealment distinguishes the animal's poverty in a world from the world-forming which characterizes man.[10]

Using Heidegger's categories that are attuned to the different states of existence shared by inanimate things and animals, Agamben means to define the man–animal divide free from the hierarchies assumed by Linnaeus's taxonomies. The key term is "disconcealment," borrowed from Heidegger's *offenbar,* (meaning obvious, apparent, but also not concealed). Agamben's interest is to find new ways to understand an animal's being as "non-related," free in its existence next to and beside humans, but not in some assumed hierarchy valued "beneath" human life. But also, importantly, Agamben seeks new ways to value the lives of animals whose mode of existence is rich in its concealed character and, now, also important to understanding what is lacking in human consciousness. For my purposes, the bare arts of proverbs, with their seeming autonomic recall, and parables and fabula of animal existence best capture the "closedness" of being that characterizes human existence in a world of stark necessity. The bare arts, then, like the buried paradoxical nature of some of the seemingly negative categories in Heidegger's philosophy, where terms like "closed" and "captivation" come to magically reveal strengths or powers now seen as possibly positive and redeeming, come to share the strength and vitality of heretofore undervalued states of existence.

The quality of prescriptive narrative, then, would not be seen as backward or "captive" to the slave existence, in Hegel's terms, but would be seen by eco-materialist Joanna Zylinska as

---

10 Giorgio Agamben, *The Open: Man and Animal,* trans. Kevin Attell (Stanford: Stanford University Press, 2004), 55.

appropriate to her understanding of "critical vitalism," "a mode of philosophical production" that is "fragmented: it gives up on any desire to forge systems, ontologies or worlds and makes itself content with minor, even if abundant, interventions into material and conceptual unfoldings."[11] I want to return to this idea of art trapped outside the self-reflective subject, "open" as Agamben might say, and made to speak to forces outside the rational in my own parable of *King Lear*. At times, Hegel suggests that this "slavish" mode of representation is free from self-conscious awareness, like that form of consciousness imagined to describe the instinct-driven life of animals or the metabolic being of the plant world. I have questions about the psychology of this model of openness. I want to think about how mnemonic language implies a subject lost in memory whose historical agency is "enmeshed" in encounters with the environment, and how these encounters are recorded, stored as vital traces of world-being left for later use, like remnants in the fault lines and rifts of striated rock sediments. But before we speak more of *Lear* as enmeshed encounter with its environment, I want to tease more at the edges of the idea of parable and bare art storytelling. If mining *Lear* for precepts required swimming against the current of modernist theories of textual dissonance, to shed our habits of value we have to come to terms with Hegel's hold on the literary aesthetics. If we want to read *Lear* as a parable about the mnemonic self — offering a view of the self buried in its own table of memory — we need to think more about the uneasy feeling we may have of doing harm to the sacred object by seeing it merely as parable, or ignoring the deeper critical valence of the art text, as the argument is made.

The description of parables trapped in their analogy would be defined as the fault limit of the narrative form for Hegel, who comments that Aesop's animals never become more than their species, as if the comparisons between the Ant as diligent or Grasshopper as imprudent never leave their animal-being at-

11 Joanna Zylinska, *Minimal Ethics for the Anthropocene* (Ann Arbor: Open Humanities Press/MPublishing, 2014), 14–15.

tributes that are somehow contained in their symbolic representation:

> The lion, for example, is taken as a symbol of magnanimity, the fox of cunning, the circle of eternity, the triangle of the Trinity. But the lion and the fox do possess in themselves the very qualities whose significance they are supposed to express.... *Therefore in these sorts of symbol the sensuously present things have already in their own existence that meaning,* for the representation and expression of which they are used; and, taken in this wider sense, the symbol is no purely arbitrary sign, but a sign which in its externality comprises in itself at the same time the content of the idea which it brings into appearance.[12]

Re-accessorizing *Lear* as a parable of the posthuman would mean to pay attention to the immersed quality, "open" in its prescriptive representation. Again, for Zylinska, this "sensuously present" affective prescript would appeal to the minimal ethics of her critical vitalism, as

> a different modulation of rationality, one that remains more attuned to its own modes of production. It is always embodied and immersed, responding to the call of matter and its various materializations — materializations such as humans, animals, plants, inanimate objects, as well as relations between them.[13]

Perhaps we could tease out even more from Hegel's view of the bare arts and their Phrygian origins. Though it is difficult to untangle one instance of Hegel's writing without feeling like it is connected in some unending strand to the rest of his entire mode of thought, Phrygia can easily be seen to function as a pivotal scene in his dialectic model. As a form of prose enslaved to

---

12 Hegel, *Aesthetics*. Emphasis mine.
13 Zylinska, *Minimal Ethics,* 15.

the real, lean arts are also home to Aesop's world, whose legendary place of residence, Phrygia, comes to symbolize the transition from body to mind, from the "attachment to nature, to the country in which man begins to apprehend the spiritual and his own self."[14] Phrygia serves in Hegel's thought as the border-territory of the Absolute, humankind's progress to a more subjective idealism. Like humanists in the Renaissance, Hegel inherits the image of Phrygia (located in the western part of Anatolia) as the home of foundational Greek legends and myths, home to Mygdon who battled the Amazons, where king Midas was to have learned his harsh lesson about gold, and where Alexander cut the Gordian knot. It is a land abundant in fables and whose very history seems indistinguishable from myth. For Hegel, Phrygia is the very cradle of prescriptive economies of narrative, but it is also the home of advanced symbolism, in a way, tangentially linked in his own model to the moment in human history where the inverse logic of "the negative" takes flight as a dialectic process. In his terms Phrygia inherits the Egyptian view toward death where mortality takes on its potent religious significance as rebirth, where "the death of what is natural" becomes "absolutely grounded in the Divine ... [and] is then compensated by rediscovery, resurrection, renewal, so that now ceremonial festivities can follow."[15] When speaking of Cybele worship in Phrygia, which "reverberates too in the myths of Castor and Pollux, Ceres and Proserpine," Hegel speaks of the birth of symbolic thought. The lacunae here is significant, because Hegel wants to say the moment of transcendental thought is one that turns its back on the prescriptive:

> [T]he form of the *human* body is a symbol, a form which appears elaborated in a higher and more appropriate way because the spirit at this stage already begins in general to give shape to itself, disengaging itself from the purely natural and rising to its own more independent existence. This

14 Hegel, *Aesthetics*.
15 Ibid.

constitutes the general nature of symbol proper and the necessity of art for its presentation. Now in order to review the
more concrete conceptions underlying this stage, we must,
in connection with this first descent of spirit into itself, leave
the East and turn rather to the West.[16]

For Hegel, Phrygia is a transitional moment of human history,
where a new form of transcendental existence seems to pick itself up and walk into Western modernity. Phrygia, then, plays a
role much like Levant does in the evolutionary histories used by
paleontologists today to tell the story of *homo sapiens*'s migration out of Africa into the rich arable lands of the northwest
Arabian plate, the crossroads of western Asia. Hegel's archeology of aesthetics can be located in this evolutionary narrative.
The Levant is this transitional territory where our story as species begins; it is the site of what paleontologists call the great
migration. "Agriculture was invented around 10,000 years ago,
in the Levant," Gaia Vince explains in her *Adventures in the Anthropocene: A Journey to the Heart of the Planet We Made,* "and
was triggered by climate change." She continues:

> After the last ice age, the [last geological era] Holocene
> ushered in warmer conditions with long dry seasons that
> favored cereals. These annual grasses could mature rapidly
> within a season, dying off to leave a dormant embryonic
> stage — a seed — that could survive the dry periods ....The
> first farmers gathered wild grains to sow around settle-
> ments, where they could be harvested, stored during times
> of plenty, dehusked and milled ....These early farmers began
> to radically change Earth's landscapes. Humans were burn-
> ing naturally occurring vegetation, such as forests, to plant
> their artificially generated varieties in easily harvestable
> zones — the first crop fields were born. At the same time as
> changing local ecology, humans were changing other bio-
> diversity by domesticating animals such as chickens, pigs,

16 Ibid.

and cows, which used the new grasslands to graze safely and provided meat, milk and manure.[17]

The Levant is where the Anthropocene begins. The Anthropocene is a term invented by Nobel laureate Paul Crutzen to describe the current geological era where humans, experiencing the fate of their ingenuity, live in an environment entirely constructed of their own making: the burning of grasses to make arable land, the use of fossil fuels and the consumption of raw materials needed for constructing large settlements eventually impacts our own species's evolution.[18]

Can we fold this narrative of Levantine-Phrygia into *King Lear*? Or, at the very least, tease out how the play's view of ancient English history seems analogous to Hegel's understanding of the "transitional" point in the archeology of aesthetics? As a narrative of human evolution and geological time, this moment is coterminous with Hegel's imagined transition from the bare art of parables and proverbs to the self-reflective and symbolic. The Anthropocene is the site where Hegel's Phrygian bare arts exist as a last remnant before being shed, a land whose plenty is beginning to free humankind from its oral tradition of parables and fables, saws and myths of regeneration, to pass on its laws and social regulations. The annual grasses provided the "surplus" of stored carbohydrates, the real "kernel" of human economic determination, to live through times of want and spend our energy on tool-making, language, religion.[19] We have seen

17 Gaia Vince, *Adventures in the Anthropocene: A Journey to the Heart of the Planet We Made* (London: Chatto and Windus, 2014), 106–7.

18 P.J. Crutzen, "Geology of mankind," *Nature* 415.6867 (Jan 3, 2002): 23.

19 I am aware that the discovery of Göbekli Tepe in Turkey overturns the archeological formula of modern human history: "first cities, then religion," as the 11,000-year-old structure predates the agricultural revolution. If I understand the debate, the argument is that pilgrimage to religious temples was the impetus for finding ways to live in larger social groups, and therefore the catalyst for early humans inventing harvesting techniques to live in urban environments. See Andrew Curry, "Gobekli Tepe: The World's First Temple?" *Smithsonian Magazine,* Nov. 2008, http://www.smithsonianmag.com/history/gobekli-tepe-the-worlds-first-temple-83613665/?no-ist

previously where Shakespeare is weighing the difference between the pharmakon of rhetorical speech and a more authen-
tic form of communication: an organic speech where we "speak
what we feel not what we ought to say." But at the same time,
Lear's characters seem to reflect on crisis and calamity through
the proverbial language out of habit, out of instinct, to survive
the day. This contradiction is the Phrygian shadow of the play's
evolutionary emergence from of its own dark age. From Shakespeare's position, the historical moment of *Lear*'s regressive fantasy of "returning" to proverbial language occurs on the heath,
where Lear lives a parable of the posthuman.

The Aesthetics of Consumption

This is not a forced reading, by any means. One could easily
argue that Shakespeare's tragedy offers a clear parable about
prodigality and living within an economy of expenditure. The
representation of domestic expense — at the heart of the play's
initial conflict between King and daughters — is one of the
"mental cognates," as Hugh Grady might say, that orients the
narrative for us living within the Anthropocene as a parable
about sustainability, scarcity, and the "superflux" of wealth (*King
Lear* 3.4.36). There is a long-standing tradition of reading *King
Lear* as Shakespeare's response to the social problem of vagrancy.[20] For an eco-materialist "shift," we might want to draw upon

20 See Linda Woodbridge's *Vagrancy, Homelessness, and English Renaissance
Literature* (Urbana and Chicago: University of Illinois Press, 2001). See also:
A.L. Beier, *Masterless Men: The Vagrancy Problem in England* (London:
Methuen, 1985); William C. Carroll, *Fat King, Lean Beggar: Representations
of Poverty in the Age of Shakespeare* (Ithaca: Cornell University Press, 1996);
Craig Dionne and Steve Mentz, ed., *Rogues and Early Modern Literary Culture* (Ann Arbor: University of Michigan Press, 2004); Patricia Fumerton,
*Unsettled: The Culture of Mobility and the Working Poor in Early Modern
England* (Chicago: University of Chicago Press, 2006); Paola Pugliatti, *Beggary and Theatre in Early Modern England* (Burlington, VT: Ashgate, 2003);
and Bryan Reynolds, *Transversal Enterprises in the Drama of Shakespeare
and his Contemporaries: Fugitive Explorations* (New York: Palgrave Macmillan, 2006). See my overview of the debates in this field in "'Now For the

this critical conversation by reframing the contrasting images of courtly indulgence and poverty in the posthuman context. Goneril's perspective of her father's train of knights tells the story of courtly extravagance. Her complaint is, in part, one of realpolitik. She sees potential insurrection in the sheer numbers of Lear's followers, "that on every dream, / Each buzz, each fancy, each complaint, dislike … may engaurd" the king's "dotage with their powers" (1.4.302–4). Lear's defense enshrines each of his knights with an idealized feudal value. From his perspective, "need" is defined according to an economy of debt and obligation that misidentifies the scale of dependence and consumption Goneril intuits. For Lear, value is determined by social obligation, and his men deserve the "effects of courtesy, dues of gratitude" (2.4.172) befitting their status, which is defined finally by the reciprocal nature of liege fealty:

> … of choice and rarest parts,
> That all particulars of duty know
> And in the most exact regard support
> The worships of their name. (1.4.240–43)

Goneril's original complaint is fraught with the domestic concerns of economic "disorder." She argues the "riotous knights" are prodigal; "Epicurism" makes her palace "more like a tavern or a brothel" (1.4.219–20). It is thus not hard to hear the theme of non-sustainable expenditure that underlies Lear's defense of his retinue. When he overvalues the worth of his vassals, he demonstrates how social values like status are predicated on aristocratic symbols of extravagant consumption (*fig.* 7).

Lear's words are concise: "effects of courtesy, dues of gratitude." What is "due" to any manor guest is carefully prescribed in the unwritten code of courtesy the sumptuary laws of the period tried unsuccessfully to enforce. Each guest would be of-

Lords' Sake': Vagrancy, Downward Mobility, and Low Aesthetics," special issue on "Vagrant Subjects," *Early Modern Culture Electronic Seminar* 7 (2008): http://emc.eserver.org/1–7/dionne_response.html.

Figure 7. Pieter Claesz, *Still Life With a Peacock Pie*, 1627.

fered the bounty of gifts (food, furnishing, and service) the sum of whose conspicuous value would symbolize the king's beneficence. Goneril's complaint could be directed at the long history of Tudor and Stuart court extravagance, if we remember the stories of Henry VIII's first colossally wasteful court, whose scale of improvidence is beyond the pale even by today's standards. Henry Tudor had to leave Hampton, as legend has it, because his kitchen routinely denuded the surrounding countryside of its livestock, fruits, and vegetables to feed his guests.[21] One of the "lost practices" of the feudal age is *courtesy,* the liberal spending of the gentle classes. Lawrence Stone calls this the "acid test" of aristocratic identity: "Money was the means of acquiring and retaining status, but it was not the essence of it." He explains, "[T]

21 King James's profligate court, surely the subtext of *Lear*'s reflection on Epicurism, differed only in degree from Henry Tudor's. Typically, James is seen as "returning" to Henry's lavish practices after Elizabeth's rather thrifty management. According to S.J. Houston, the extravagant feasts and masques of James I were infrequent, but no less expensive, considered a necessary expense of maintaining the difference between the "courtesy of the aristocracy" (spending liberally) and the "mystique" of the liberal monarch (spending beyond the pale). "The Court had to be magnificent enough to impress foreign envoys and beguile prospective office-holders." *James I* (London: Routledge, 1973; reprinted 2014), 16.

he acid test was the mode of life, a concept that involved many factors. Living on a private income was one, but more important was spending liberally, dressing elegantly, and entertaining lavishly."[22] In his opus *The Crisis of the Aristocracy,* a core section entitled "Conspicuous Consumption" maps out his central thesis that the ruling class in the sixteenth century viewed identity in ways counter to a post-Reformation frame of reference, where in Western cultures the accumulation of wealth became an indicator of status.[23] In fact, the opposite is the case for early modern England: "[T]his was an age of exceptionally prodigal living, made possible by the rising tide of luxury imports and stimulated by a desire to imitate the opulent Renaissance courts of Europe. Tastes which found favor with a Medici prince were sedulously copied by a less richly endowed English earl."[24] Stone's description of the "economic incentive" to this culture of emulating the European peerage could be read as the animating dialectic of the aesthetics of consumption:

> In the abnormally fluid situation of the late sixteenth and early seventeenth centuries, with large numbers of relatively new families pouring into the gentry, the knightage, the baronetage, and the peerage, the struggles of the status-seekers were particularly violent. The enormous inflation by King James in the numbers of all ranks in itself greatly increased the incentive to spend more freely, "men of honor being not seldom compelled to proportion their layings out to their dignitaries, not their port to their ability." A self-perpetuat-

22 Lawrence Stone, *The Crisis of the Aristocracy, 1558–1641* (Oxford: Oxford University Press, 1965), 50.

23 Stone is often read as applying Thorstein Veblen's model because of his use of this term, but the majority of Veblen's insights apply to a capitalist acquisitive culture. Veblen's idea of "pecuniary emulation," for example, describes a class where "the possession of wealth, which was at the outset valued simply as an evidence of efficiency, becomes in popular apprehension, itself a meritorious act. Wealth is now itself intrinsically honorable and confers honor on its possessor." Veblen, *The Theory of the Leisure Class* (1899) (New Brunswick: Transaction Publishers, 1992), 22.

24 Stone, *The Crisis of the Aristocracy,* 184.

ing cycle was thus set up. Over-consumption led to sale of land, which generated social mobility and psychological insecurity among the purchasers; in its turn insecurity caused a struggle for status, exacerbated by the inflation of honors, which found expression in competitive consumption.[25]

Peter Burke's fascinating account of the Italian aristocracy, *The Historical Anthropology of Early Modern Italy: Essays on Perception and Communication,* traces Stone's study of the reckless consumption back to its source, in a word, showing the Italian exemplars of decadence upon which the English modeled their status (Burke uses the testimony of travelers to Italy, including Montaigne).[26] Burke's anthropological analysis uses the example of the Kwakiutl peoples of the Vancouver area, famous in a range of anthropological and ethnographic studies for their extremely competitive traditions, and the way they devised "fighting with property." "The characteristic expression of Kwakiutl emulation," Burke explains, "was the now celebrated 'potlatch,' a meeting of rivals at which they destroyed their two main forms of wealth, blankets and copper plates, taunting their opponents to do the same. Participants," he continues, "thus showed their contempt for the property destroyed, humiliated competitors who were unable to follow suit, and so converted wealth into prestige."[27] That Burke finds a cornerstone analogue in the Kwakiutl potlatch to think about the scale of the Italian aristocracy's consumption tells a great deal about the stakes of the game for the Italian nobility: "For families who had already arrived at the summit, conspicuous consumption was regarded as a duty....It was necessary to avoid shame, in other words loss of face, to sustain a high position of the honor of the house."[28] When Burke looks to what exactly is being consumed, he con-

25 Ibid., 185.
26 Peter Burke, *The Historical Anthropology of Early Modern Italy: Essays on Perception and Communication* (Cambridge: Cambridge University Press, 2005).
27 Ibid., 132.
28 Ibid., 134.

firms Stone's original analysis of the most important costs in maintaining one's status in the competition to purchase honor through waste: "building, food, clothes, transport, funerals, and tombs, *in that order*."[29]

In his book *The Banquet: Dining in the Great Courts of Late Renaissance Europe,* Ken Albala documents the changing tastes of the elite courts and their chefs from the late medieval to the early modern period. In general, there is a broad shift during this time toward the eating of domesticated animals, based on economic trends, "A rising demand for food resulting from demographic pressure," he explains,

> can only have been met by increasing output and cultivating or grazing more land. There was also a greater percentage of the population living in cities, and more legal restrictions on hunting and collecting food in the wild. Ultimately there was a more dependable supply of cultivated plants and domesticated animals, particularly in Northern Europe."[30]

Albala imagines that this macro-level shift is only partly dependent on what we might term the Annales School's emphasis on large-scale trends of production, and colonization of the New World and the introduction of slave labor and Eastern trade, particularly with spices, like sugar and cinnamon.[31] "These factors cannot be discounted, but there are other equally interesting cultural reasons for a shift," he avers.

> The change in mentality may have been triggered by material factors, or one could say conversely that a new relationship to nature and the willingness to subdue and master it for the benefit of humans is what ultimately led

29 Ibid., 137. Emphasis mine.
30 Ken Albala, *The Banquet: Dining in the Great Courts of Late Renaissance Europe* (Chicago: University of Illinois Press, 2007), 33.
31 The French school of history in the twentieth century placed emphasis on long term social history. Co-founders of the school include Luicen Febvre (1878–1956), Henri Hauser (1866–1946), and March Bloch (1866–1944).

to the economic and social changes. This is a matter of the ideological chicken or material egg. Whichever, there was a reduction of the number and variety of wild foods normally consumed by Europeans between the Late Middle Ages and the eighteenth century.[32]

But against this broader shift, the aristocracy's rush to maintain status seems to react in the opposite direction: the elite taste for wild game and the variety of food at the banquet table seems to explode, as wild food becomes more and more a commodity symbol for refined taste. Albala attends to the banquet as part of the elaborate game of maintaining status relations. The practice of "dining" is at the center of aristocratic displays of status:

> Consider the message intended by an aristocratic hunter who invites his social inferior to partake in his catch. The exchange, while ostensibly displaying friendship, may also be reinforcing deference, dependence, and mutual obligation. The key lies in the context. Serving a guest a food widely regarded as an aphrodisiac sends a different kind of message if in an intimate setting. Ordering an outlandish and highly spiced dish to be shared among friends can, again depending on the context, be intended as a challenge to see who has the most daring palate. Those who can withstand the hottest or most revolting food have affirmed their superiority over those who have bowed out. This is, even if in sublimated form, a reenactment of basic hard-wired rutting instincts. In fact, in each of these examples, the meal re-stages, if you will, a central human drive to dominate, to woo, to challenge. Each is also a kind of play.[33]

Albala's notions of human domination aside, his careful reading of the cookbooks and dining guidebooks of the early modern period offers perhaps one of the most succinct portraits of the

32 Albala, *The Banquet,* 33.
33 Ibid., 4.

grand scale of courtly banquets as part of the untold theater of Renaissance self-fashioning. Exotic meats and exquisitely spiced dishes were part of the high theater of the court, using food as a way to parade status, but also as a means to win over one's guests not, as the adage goes, through their hearts but through their stomachs. The patron's wealth and prestige was made viscerally concrete in a tableau of smells and tastes. As Albala argues, the other forms of courtly address could be seen as merely incidental to the meal itself. "The table was one of the primary routes of patronage," he explains. He continues:

> Thus a prince was sending a message not only to his guests and foreign dignitaries but to his courtly staff, and even to the general public when they were invited to gawk. Everything was an elaborate performance in cooking, serving, and eating. It was also a mummery or "dumb show" for the real power relations that took place outside the banquet hall. In a ritualistic form the unequal status of the diners was enacted in the seating arrangements, and especially in who was invited to serve whom. Patronage networks were in silent form made perfectly clear, perhaps even more so than with a modern corporate management flowchart that only graphically represents subordination. Here it is acted out for everyone to see.[34]

The exquisite dishes of the banquet were meant to cater to the refined taste of the Renaissance gentleman, who learned to appreciate the finer balance of spices. Domesticated food still appears on the table: pork, lamb, beef. But also wildfowl: pigeons, doves, peacocks, guinea hens, turkeys from the New World, pheasant, quail, fig-peckers, sparrows, weld ducks, teals, and tiny thrushes. And fish: eels, oysters, and copious shellfish. "Although vast quantities of food are still fashionable," Albala notes, "we also know fine food when we see it."[35] Parsley, fennel, elder, borage,

34   Ibid., 7.
35   Ibid., 9.

and violets. "Spices and sugar in particular, in copious doses — one would never want to seem tight-fisted with them — not only proclaim the lengths a person will go to flavor food but are also the most conspicuous form of consumption."[36] Wild herbs: cresses, skirrets, samphire, holly roots, water caltrops, nettles, mallows and wild onions. Albala's history of aristocratic eating practices can read to the ecologist like a gruesome chronology of expenditure. But he pulls no punches in tracing the haunted cravings of the patrician class whose attempts at reasserting status in the face of economic changes reached a harried crescendo in refined tastes:

> One particularly perverse fashion among the elites involved removing the unborn fetus of a deer and cooking it. "This was invented either by gluttonous men or to be something elegant, not because it's pleasant or healthy, but uncommon and acquired at a high price," claimed Delmenico Sala. Petrus Castellanus attests to the same fashion and adds that young stags' horns have also become popular as delicacies on noble tables, just when they begin to poke through. Normally they were boiled and the soft interior removed and served, or they were grated and boiled to make hartshorn jelly. Most of these references come from seventeenth-century dietary works, and they usually condemn practices they found aberrant or unhealthy. They do suggest, however, that these wild foods were disappearing or were only eaten in extremely remote places or by courtly gluttons with jaded palates and a taste for the perverse. They do not appear at all in the elite banquets by the seventeenth century, but had in earlier cookbooks. That is, in the court of these centuries small furry creatures went from viable, if rare, menu items to strange and perverse foods.[37]

---

36 Ibid., 3.
37 Ibid., 36.

Figure 8. Pieter Claesz, *Still Life With a Turkey Pie,* 1627.

Albala never shifts his attention from cookbooks and dining guides, but he does reference comparable aesthetic styles of poetry and painting in the "baroque" attention to fine detail of the presentation of the food, "much like the attention to lavish ingredients used in baroque architecture: colored marble, and especially gold and silver … [were both used] in decoration of building and food."[38] The central dishes presented in each course are huge *tableaux vivants* of one main ingredient surrounded by a profusion of garnishes."There is still," he concludes, "far too much food for mortals to consume, and it is still served on a monumental scale."[39]

One is tempted to follow Albala's hint, then, and read this opulence through the Dutch still-life painting tradition, which retroactively fixes for the modern eye the sumptuousness of aristocratic courtesy through the post-Reformation lens of frugality and cost. In the early seventeenth-century tabletop paintings of Pieter Claesz or Willem Kalf, the naturalist rendering of delicacies is arranged to provide an image of the neglected serving table after the feast: a pie half-eaten, oysters untouched, overturned glasses, and flasks of wine opened but unpoured. As

38 Ibid., 23.
39 Ibid., 23.

Figure 9. Frans Snyders, *The Pantry*, 1640.

the genre progressed, the medieval symbol of the skull as *momento mori* was inserted on these tabletop renderings to remind the reader of the obvious. From our vantage point, the interest is in the careless expenditure signified in the image of the discarded food as a vision of wasted beauty, an undervalued but aesthetically rich item now meant to signify through the translation of the decadent natural hues a newly discovered courtly dissipation (*fig.* 8).

Can we hear a similar incipient concern for decadence in Lear's confrontation with Goneril? It is not hard to see the love test at the beginning of the play as happening after the banquet itself. But such literalizing of the play overlooks the tragedy's deeper preoccupation with the theme of dissipation. The history of excessive manor house hosting sits under the strained encounter. We should remind ourselves of the actual statistics. One of the incidental things a tourist today learns when visiting Hampton Court Palace in East Molesey, Surrey, is the particular history of the palace kitchens and the staggering quantities of provisions offered Henry VIII's guests. Though we have access to first-hand accounts of the King James's spectacular masques, which read like screeds against libertine excess, today's antiquarian preservationists of England's Historic Royal Palaces keep alive the material history of the management from behind the scenes, as it were, of the court kitchens, and the ecological cost of the grandiose scale of consumption first witnessed by the English as its monarchs imported the continental customs of *noblesse oblige*. Henry's court entitled 600 people to eat twice a day, and its "annual provision for meat for the Tudor court stood at 1,240 oxen, 8,200 sheep, 2,330 deer, 760 calves, 1,870 pigs and 53 wild boar."[40] Walking through the labyrinth of the kitchen and connecting hallways today, one can see the various slaughtering benches and blood troughs next to the serving windows and banquet tables. The King could only entertain for a couple of weeks at a time, one is told, before the local farmers and shepherds felt the strain of this consumption. Thus the monarch's "progress" was born as a response to unsustainable manorial custom, a kind of grotesque mirror image of the beggar's nomadic life. *Lear*'s grandiose redemptive gestures are not removed from this Anthropocenic logic, as his own journey over the heath turns this spectacle into a tableau of just desserts as the king is made to follow a beggar's progress across the scorched earth of his own making (*fig.* 9).

Lear's narrative about the decline of feudal values and manorial custom — service, honor, paternal devotion — employs images of social decay and chaos to evoke a similarly affective excess of the strongest possible empathy toward its lost world. The play laments the disappearance of these ideals through their tragic negligence and abuse: fathers and devoted children and servants are the object of the play's most hysterical or frenetic sympathies. The virtuous and honorable characters are subject to a kind of Renaissance version of a theater of cruelty, the "counter-logic" of over-valued sentiment meant to stir the most intense compassions, as these characters are ritualistically ban-

40 "Henry VIII's Kitchens," *Historic Royal Palaces: Hampton Court Palace,* http://www.hrp.org.uk/HamptonCourtPalace/stories/thetudorkitchens.

ished, tortured, and murdered; where we witness manor-hosts and servants paid back in a cruel "inverse" economy a torturous tribute for their generosity.

Can we think of Shakespeare's tragedy, then, as a kind of sympathy machine working according to the logic of manor house consumption? Within the human, a combination of psychosomatic triggers are effected by the portrayal of suffering, what cognitive and behavioral psychologists call "contextual appraisal and modulation" (sensory images of anxiety or emotion in others) that, in turn, lead to "emotional contagion."[41] Such an event is precisely the kind of assemblage discussed in eco-materialist frames to theorize agency working across a range of macro- and micro-contexts within and without a lived environment. In perhaps the first psychological appraisal of Shakespeare's theater by François Guizot in 1852, we read "the very nature of dramatic poetry" defined in strikingly similar terms:

> Its power rests upon the effects of sympathy — of that mysterious force which causes laughter to beget laughter, which bids tears to flow at the sight of tears, and which, in spite of the diversity of dispositions, conditions, and characters, produces the same impression on all upon whom it simultaneously acts.[42]

On the early modern stage, the smells of the sweaty wool stockings, the ambient sounds of rushed footsteps across food planks, the anxious breath of the actors and the spittle from their mouth as they project their voices, the emotional pitch of their voices: a symbiosis of cues that affect anxiety and wrap the shrill words with enough of an emotional realism to activate the autonomic response needed to identify with the narrative's representation of trauma. The story of Lear's progress on the heath would trig-

---

41 Frederique Vignemont and Tania Singer, "The Empathic Brain: How, When and Why?" *Trends in Cognitive Sciences* 10.10 (2006): 437–39 [435–41].

42 François Pierre Guillaume Guizot, *Shakespeare and His Times* (New York: Harper and Brothers, 1852), 6.

ger a "shared emotional network," psychologists today might say, a semantic context representing an identifiable experience familiar to the viewer, allowing for complex combinations of sensory and cognitive processes ("similarity between the empathizer's and the target's experiential repertoires").[43] The result is a kind of spreading "contagion" of sympathy for a culture of expenditure: the audience made zombies who are "bitten" by the strong emotional affect of the play's ideological hold and made to identify with the class largely responsible for the scarcity they encounter when they exit the theater.[44]

But the contagion of sympathy spreads because of the way we are made. As a species, the ability to identify with others, what early evolutionary psychologists called "reciprocal altruism," the ability to empathize with kin, family, and strangers who can aid in labor involved in hunting and gathering, increased our chances of survival and, over time and through natural selection, this trait defined the human.[45] Such an "immersed" view of tragedy's impulse to initiate the audience into a ritualized spectacle of fate (Lear's "wheel of fire") speaks to what evolutionary psychology might describe as our species's predilection toward sympathetic identification. There is no reason we cannot historicize theorized "inherited traits" in this way. We need not toss away historicism when rushing to science to explain the affec-

43 Vignemont and Singer, "The Empathic Brain," 439..

44 To continue with the *World War Z* analogy (dir. Marc Foster, Paramount Pictures, 2013), the zombie in the throes of the affective charge of the emotion represented on the stage leaves the theater with an empathetic connection to the superfluity of the Anthropocene.

45 The evolutionary psychology is not without its contradictions (see my comments below on humans being "out of phase" with inherited communal traits), but it is not an overstatement to say that the discourse envisions humans as born sympathetic sponges, or melodramatic primates, as it were, predisposed to reciprocal altruism, more likely than not to be constructed by insistent images that "hail" us, address us from a position of empathetic necessity. See Robert L. Trivers, "The Evolution of Reciprocal Altruism," *The Quarterly Review of Biology* 46.1 (1971): 35–57; and W.D. Hamilton, "The Genetical Evolution of Social Behavior," *Journal of Theoretical Biology* 7 (1964): 1–52.

tive level of the text and the "instincts" shared as humans.[46] In this instance, *King Lear* means to elicit our sympathies for those who represent a traditional hierarchy, symbols of age-old practices of feudal production: the benevolent gift-givers associated with manor-house customs and property, the patriarch's establishment of lines of issue and inheritance, the rights and obligations of *rentier* — "hosting" of guests at court and manor — the dues of "courtesy" and "honor" of lesser aristocracy. *Lear* is a sympathy machine that molds the "contextual appraisal" around a concrete set of social practices that are, from Shakespeare's early seventeenth-century perspective, from the dim past of demesne production and liege relations.[47]

And the machine is set full tilt. The play works against itself in this curious way. The tragedy's zeal to ennoble its nostalgic past is a poetic strategy caught up in the very logic of aristocratic display, a social class whose most significant status marker, as we have discussed, is that of reckless spending and wasteful prodigality. *King Lear*'s treatment of these "dying" social values is co-

---

46 I would argue that the over-emphasis on a "universal" instinctive "man" is a typical humanist reading of science. See Joseph Carrol's reading of the "universal human compassion" and use of "sympathy" in the evolutionary model of "An Evolutionary Approach to Shakespeare's *King Lear,*" *Critical Insights: Family,* ed. John Knapp (Ipswich: EBSCO, 2012): 83–103. In a compelling general overview of the play, Carrol's description of the evolutionary model aligns a determinist-essentialist view of "human nature" with a rather traditional humanist reading of *Lear*. This is read in his approach to characters as depoliticized figures that reinforce "'normative universals' and reinforce adaptive mechanisms." "In literatures across the world, more often than not, antagonists are actuated chiefly by a desire for power and personal gain; protagonists tend to form prosocial clusters by helping kin, creating friendship groups and exercising magnanimity toward the less fortunate" (92).

47 My idea of a sympathy machine overlaps with Catherine Silverstone's finally more nuanced argument of "ethical spectatorship" in *Shakespeare, Trauma and Contemporary Performance* (London: Routledge, 2011), especially her description of how "performances of Shakespeare's texts and their documentary traces work variously to memorialize, remember and witness violent events and histories, but … these processes are never neutral. Performances offer a way of remembering violent events and histories and invite spectators to witness theses events" (3–4).

terminous with the extravagant expenditure in its over-valuing of the receding past. Even though the play means to celebrate the aristocratic class virtues, its "regress towards a fantasized rebirth of feudal values"[48] is its own improvident performative gesture, a representational strategy whose "consumption" vortex works like an unseen gravitational force to spin even its own redemptive ideals into its maw. Our passions are manipulated around scenes of inflated cruelty. The tragedy's excessive strategy to control the audience's interests works to pay back the loss of generosity where our sympathies are extravagantly "consumed" like so much lamb pastry. Richard Halpern describes this as a kind of reckless self-divestiture, an "aristocratic *depense*":

> To say that Lear attempts to revive the values of the feudal aristocracy, and that to this end it narrates in reverse a certain version of the transition to capitalist society, may create the false impression that it is a nostalgic play and that its tragic vision results from a consciousness of the impossibility of its historical project. But this is to mistake the matter entirely. The play does not passively watch the collapse of a social order which it portrays. It throws this order — or its declining values — over the edge, consumes it in a massive act of *depense*. It thus reconstitutes through destruction. *King Lear* is, then, no more nostalgic for what is lost than someone watching a waterfall is nostalgic for the lake above. The destruction of the characters in increasingly costly warfare means not that a social structure is being torn apart but that it is being reconstituted in a tragic form. To be thrown over the edge is not, after all, the same as being rent asunder: it is, rather, to achieve a perfect momentary state of equipoise, as even the force of gravity seems to be canceled in the seconds before impact.[49]

48 Richard Halpern, *The Poetics of Primitive Accumulation: English Renaissance Culture and the Genealogy of Capital* (Ithaca: Cornell University Press, 1991), 269.

49 Ibid.

Critics have approached the question for a long time, almost since the inception of the original play: what is the source of Shakespeare's fatalism? A.C. Bradley's famous description of Lear's skepticism can be heard behind Halpern's. While defining what Bradley saw as the ineffable greatness of Shakespeare's tragic characters, he posited that there is still a "tragic impression" that lingers:

> And with this greatness of the tragic hero (which is not always confined to him) is connected, secondly, what I venture to describe as the center of the tragic impression. This central feeling is the impression of waste. With Shakespeare, at any rate, the pity and fear which are stirred by the tragic story seem to unite with, and even to merge in, a profound sense of sadness and mystery, which is due to this impression of waste. "What a piece of work is man," we cry; "so much more beautiful and so much more terrible than we knew! Why should he be so if this beauty and greatness only tortures itself and throws itself away?" We seem to have before us a type of the mystery of the whole world, the tragic fact which extends far beyond the limits of tragedy. Everywhere, from the crushed rocks beneath our feet to the soul of man, we see power, intelligence, life and glory, which astound us and seem to call for our worship. And everywhere we see them perishing, devouring one another and destroying themselves, often with dreadful pain, as though they came into being for no other end.[50]

Bradley's description of the fruitlessness of life as depicted in *Lear* is formative for generations of scholars who used Shakespeare's nihilism to ponder the horrors of twentieth century history. For me, Bradley's critical take of the paradox of wastefulness in *Lear* stages Shakespearean tragedy as a site to voice skepticism toward Progressivism's secular promise of a culture

---

50 A.C. Bradley, *Shakespearean Tragedy: Lectures on Hamlet, Othello, King Lear, Macbeth* (London: Macmillan, 1905), 23.

whose faith in science and industry will provide an enlightened and unified society.[51] Halpern could be said to augment or finesse this original insight made by Bradley. What makes Halpern's reading of Shakespeare's account of human wastefulness so original, though, is his insight into Shakespeare's *participation* with the reckless energy to consume its world, a seemingly dispassionate, if not borderline pathological, torching of the huts. Halpern's analysis could be said to historicize the profound fatalism of the play that works in tandem with the self-destructive delirium that defines aristocracy's profligacy.

I want to move from these critical interpretations of Lear's profligate economy to the Anthropocene. Again, when considering the context of this skepticism, we are drawn back to the play's image of expenditure. *King Lear*'s image of human need works to reproduce this aesthetics of consumption. If humans are in need of "social relations" — modern historicism's own atrociously inhuman term for things like friendship, love, respect — then this need is pictured in *King Lear* in its starkest terms, its portrayal on the stage subjected to the same manic energy, thrown into relief in the barest of settings. We are given brief glimpses of it in lightning flashes in front of hovels, among the sheepfolds, on the steaming blood-soaked ground after a battle, in front of wearied soldiers and assassins, before it too is tossed away as an afterthought. If there is anything redemptive in these images, the very faith we might have in its possibility seems like one of the horrifying strategies of the teasing gods who play with us like flies.

Lear's great set speech, "Reason not the need" and its reference to "basest beggars" is a response, we must remember, to

51 See Terry Eagleton's withering analysis of Bradley's "Victorian notions of inexorable physical laws, which if breached will exact their deadly retribution." "In the end," Eagleton continues, "Bradley throws in the towel ....Tragedy is simply tragedy, and there is nothing more to be said ....After all his conceptual twistings, Bradley can finally muster nothing more than a resounding tautology. A lengthy process of analysis is finally thrown to the winds with a saving allusion to mystery. It is the last refuge of a sophist." *Sweet Violence: The Idea of the Tragic* (New York: Wiley-Blackwell, 2002), 136.

Figure 10: Sophia Schorr-Kon, *Delphine's Call,* 2012.
Photo courtesy of Sophia Schorr-Kon.

Goneril's argument against wasteful domestic management.[52] In this context, Lear's own defense of this lifestyle seems deliberately tuned to a logic of excess, as its prickly tone and outrageous analogies is one with the excessive scale of the class it means to defend:

> O, reason not the need! Our basest beggars
> Are in the poorest thing superfluous.
> Allow not nature more than nature needs,
> Man's life's as cheap as beasts. (2.4.259–62)

Connecting the ethical dots in the analogy has always been a rhetorical challenge for literary humanists. "Kings are peo-

---

52 See Stuart Appleby, *Famine in Stuart and Tudor England* (Stanford: Stanford University Press, 1978).

ple too,"[53] the passage suggests. Allow them this one trifle, this one little "extra," a furred gown, a symbol of their humanity, a hundred knights … an Imperial fleet, another nation, the New World. None of it "nature needs," in the strictest sense, Lear asserts. The very words "Why, nature needs not what thou gorgeous wearest" (2.4.264) are often seen as the crux of the secular humanist ethos of the play, defining the human as that determined by symbolic rather than base or nutritional needs. Lear's declamation can be read through an eco-materialist lens by forcing the analogy behind the assertion: not that kings are human, but that humans are really animal in the first place. Like Lear's leveraging of his knights' "merit" as an ideological rationalization of the sumptuous consumption of his court, here too we see Lear striving to explain opulence as natural to the human. This takes for granted, from our perspective perhaps, consumer society's troubling misrecognition of inessential needs as potently vital, where the superfluous is naturalized as "essential." This is a patent ideological representation of humans as mystically (in the sense of being unspeakably so) different from the animal. In this instance, we differ only in the scale of our regard and consumption of others, what makes us equate the superfluous inhuman difference in any list of things (a hundred knights, servants, beggar, friend, France, bastard, Dover, eyes … a daughter) is that in the Anthropocene exchange value can make all of these "things" relatively equivalent, all bought or sold or tossed away for a price. Lear articulates this realization as *paralepsis,* but the statement expresses an attitude toward other life upon which the Anthropocene depends for its scale of production: "Man's life's as cheap as beast's" (2.4.262) (*fig.* 10).

Lear returns to this admission when he makes evident the man–animal nexus in his threat to abandon the terms of his daughter's deal: deny me this inexplicable "need" or I choose to live with the animals: "Return to her, and fifty men dismissed?" Lear responds, "No, rather I abjure all roofs, and choose / To wage against the enmity o' the air; / To be comrade with the

53 Hell, even the Dalai Lama wears a Rolex.

wolf and owl" (2.4.202–5). To live with the predatory wolf, or the nocturnal raptor. The play defends need as both immediately identifiable *but something that cannot be articulated.* "But, for true need —," Lear breaks off (2.4.265). It is one of the strange ironies of the play, which voices so much skepticism about the distribution of wealth and the plight of the vagrant classes, that in this set speech Lear defines "the human" as the need for *ines-sential* things.

Do we really find an answer here about what defines us? This set speech is the pivot point in the tragedy's ideological defense of the human, and it seems more than anything to articulate human need as a mystical thing, only self-evident in its absence.[54] This assertion "but, for true need —" is the obscene kernel to Lear's humanist assertion, equal to the "I'll know it when I see it" paradox of pornography, especially in the way it constitutes the object as essence only defined in a Derridean relatedness to what is deferred: *to be* is *to be* comrade with beasts, wolves, owls. What does Shakespeare mean by this caesura? The dash in Lear's line: " — "? Are we to sense that Lear is buried in thought? Thinking of his daughter Cordelia? Such silences, it has been argued, are moments where Shakespeare invents a dramatic mode of representation to signify inwardness, the immediacy of thought or unconscious motivation, where we glimpse like the dolphin's fin flashing here and there a mind somewhere, "under," beneath the surface of the words.[55] Is Lear thinking of a proverb to communicate what seems obvious to him? That hu-

---

54 See Jonathan Dollimore's succinct overview of the Christian and humanist "essentialisms" and their different responses to *King Lear* in his "*King Lear* and Essentialist Humanism," *Radical Tragedy: Religion, Ideology, and Power in the Drama of Shakespeare and his Contemporaries* (Chicago: University of Chicago Press, 1984), 189–203. Dollimore explains that the mystification of nature is precisely the function of humanism: "it mystifies suffering and invests man with a quasi-transcendent identity" (190).

55 Stephen Greenblatt's thinking about Shakespeare's "aesthetic strategy" of evoking inwardness by representing a character going through the immediacy of thought — in his words, "an intense representation of inwardness called forth by a new technique of radical excision." "The Death of Hamnet and the Making of Hamlet," *The New York Review of Books,* October 21,

mans need more than just the bare minimum to survive? Symbols, love, or recognition? But this would force Lear to acknowledge his dependence on others. This would explain the reason he cannot finish his sentence.[56] I think Lear is going through his memory for a way to communicate the wisdom needed to see the obvious truth: "why, for true need ... ." What he might find there is a storehouse of common saws on wisdom and where it comes from: "Poverty has drawn wisdom as her lot," Erasmus explains. "The belly's a great teacher of craftsmanship, / Bestower of brains ... Harsh hunger is the teacher of many men."[57] Lear's caught in mid-sentence because he knows his wisdom is acquired neither through hunger nor attrition. If Lear's language works according to the analogy of the dolphin's fin, it complicates the idea that the spontaneous free associations and silent pauses are moments where the playwright reflects on "the human" in dramatic form. In this instance the human may be as autonomic as Agamben's "open," an animal existence posited as closed to the relational world of being, a mind-as-tablet reeling through rote and potentially recalled saws now become instinctual, touchstones of wisdom through inculcated maxims. Lear pauses to articulate the self-evident truth that cannot be expressed about the human.

In the Renaissance, the adage used to articulate the irony of speaking the self-evident was "to carry wood to the forest" or "to bring water to the sea." Both images rely on the idea of the superfluous (and tangentially, the impoverished) as the link to the central metaphor, giving to someone what they already have.

2004, http://www.nybooks.com/articles/archives/2004/oct/21/the-death-of-hamnet-and-the-making-of-hamlet/.

56 Stanley Cavell has made similar claims about Lear's silent gestures. In *Disowning Knowledge in Seven of Shakespeare's Plays* (Cambridge: Cambridge University Press, 2003), he has argued persuasively that tragedy hinges on Lear's avoidance of love, which Cavell in turn sees as the Christian parable that sits at the center of the play. Cavell's argument hinges on the idea that Lear's motive is to repress this truth, to avoid the truth of his dependence.

57 "*Paupertas sapientiam sportia est,*" in *Collected Works of Erasmus: Adages: II1 to IV100,* ed. Margaret Phillips and R.A.B. Mynors (Toronto: University of Toronto Press, 1982), 401.

Erasmus makes it clear: "To carry wood to the forest is to wish to supply someone with things of which he already has a large supply."[58] The idea is that you need not communicate to someone who already lives in an abundance of knowledge. Lear would have to use proverbs of excess and lack to make his claim about human emotional need. The image is bound to the extravagant and sumptuous world of aristocratic prodigality. To articulate the self-evident, we must bring food to this already abundantly set table. At the moment where we want to see Shakespeare depicting the human in the deep gap of thought we find a moment of rote circularity, where Lear is recalling the world of want and privation flashing before his eyes.

Nonetheless, in this scene we do get a concrete definition of the *value* of the human when parsing the difference implied in Lear's statement, "man's life *is* cheap as beasts." But still, it depends on what your definition of is *is,* really, the curious divide between metaphor and metonymy. If the verb "is" works as metaphor, then humans are *like* animals and we experience our difference as a kind of symbolic remainder, a difference that we can hold on to, like the fox fur we "gorgeous wearest." If "is" functions metonymically, then what defines us is that we stand in for — can be substituted for in our radical equivalence with — the animal. Lear leaves the argument to wander wayward in the Phrygian half-light of the Anthropocene, desiring to articulate an absolute symbolics of human immanence, but seemingly bound in its relatedness to beasts in the bare world.

Cheap as Beasts: Lear's Flat Ontology

> The recognition that adaptive specializations have been shaped by the statistical features of ancestral environments is especially important in the study of human behavior ... Human psychological mechanisms should be adapted to those environments, not necessarily to ... the industrialized world.

58   Erasmus, *Adages,* 105.

— L. Cosmides and J. Tooby, "From Evolution to
  Behavior"[59]

The heath of Shakespeare's time is gone. The landlords
fenced it, put it down in furrows and grass and set the
masterless men to work upon it for wages. Lighted high-
ways were pushed through its darkness, and the King's
peace was spread like a seamless cover on the land. At
night, the police patrol its wastes. The vagrants are in
the shelters or the unemployment rolls. Old men whom
their daughters abandon now get their pension and a
home visitor.
— Michael Ignatieff, *The Needs of Strangers*[60]

If Shakespeare stages moments where Lear retreats to the adage
for survival, it is staged in a fully realized location, away from
the abundance of the court and its excesses of splendor and re-
past. *King Lear*'s heath is where the king must face the essence
of the human, where the logic of retribution plays its dark game
of defining existence against the inexplicable indifference to being. On the heath we discover a world of want and scarcity, a
place where survival means coming to terms with what makes
all humans equivalent in the most radical sense, by showing us
"unaccommodated" existence — that is, precisely *without* those
symbols of status Lear posed as the essence of human identity.[61] "The night comes on," Gloucester complains to Regan after she has watched her father leave his manor, "and the bleak
winds / Do sorely ruffle. For miles about / There's scarce a bush"
(3.295–97). The heath seems to host few objects (at least in terms

59 Cosmides and Tooby, "From Evolution to Behavior: Evolutionary Psychol-
    ogy as the Missing Link," in *The Latest and The Best Essays on Evolution and
    Optimality*, ed. J. Dupre (Cambridge: MIT Press, 1987), 280–81.
60 Michael Ignatieff, *The Needs of Strangers* (New York: Picador Macmilan,
    2001), 50.
61 Michael H. Keefer covers the different meanings of "unaccommodated" in
    "Accommodation and Synecdoche: Calvin's God in *King Lear*," *Shakespeare
    Studies* 20 (1988): 147–68.

of shelter) but many elemental forces — "fretful wind," "curled waters," "impetuous blasts," a "fury" of "to-and-fro conflicting wind and rain" (3.1.11). The force of this tempest tests the very instinctual impulse of animals to hunt for food, forcing "cub-drawn bears" (who starve from giving suck to their young) "to couch" and keep from foraging. "The lion and the belly-pinched wolf" would rather stay safe, "keep their fur dry" than hunt to survive (3.1.4–10). On the heath, then, life force is tested and our most basic instincts challenged. Stripped of their identity and history, Edgar, Lear, and Gloucester must discern what forces are at work that effect their present conditions and how their place is determined by seemingly hidden powers and agents that expose them to painful moments of self-discovery.

The heath is counter to the sumptuous court and the aristocratic identity defined by Lawrence Stone above. Rather than perform status through expenditure, one survives by taking shelter from the elements and by hiding from others. A withdrawing in rather than a laying out. To survive here one has to meld into the background, become one with the scene, hide among untouchable beggars who are only invisible because ubiquitous:

> I will preserve myself...
> To take the basest and most poorest shape...
> The country gives me proof and precedent
> Of Bedlam beggars, who, with roaring voices,
> Strike in their numbed and mortified bare arms
> Pins, wooden pricks, nails, sprigs of rosemary;
> And with this horrible object, from low farms,
> Poor pelting villages, sheep-cotes, and mills,
> Sometime with lunatic bans, sometime with prayers,
> Enforce their charity. (2.3.6–19)

Edgar is forced to "eat the swimming frog, the toad, the tadpole, the wall-newt ... [I]n the fury of his heart," he reflects oddly in the third person, "Poor Tom ... eats cow-dung for sallets, swallows the old rat and ditch-dog; drinks the green mantle of the

standing pool" (3.4.19–23). Edgar's description of this low subjectivity[62] reinforces the Elizabethan stereotype of the "sturdy
beggar," someone who was thought to fake their injuries in order to legally qualify for charity under the draconian poor laws
of the day. Shakespeare intuits that those who fake being homeless in order to beg are, finally, indiscernible from the actual
poor. Imposters of abject status live the reality of their effects.[63]

Steve Mentz has recently interpreted the storm in *King Lear*
through an eco-critical lens to account for the way the scene
offers an "alternative to dualistic notions of the self-nature relationship." Mentz suggests "*King Lear*'s opaque world of catastrophe and crisis bears an uncomfortable resemblance to the
place in which we are learning to live now. In our estranged and
estranging world," he continues,

> Lear's tortured theatre of endurance and disillusion may
> come to rival or re-write older temptations to live "in" or
> "with" nature. Such fictions about what nature is and what it
> does to our bodies may not support hopes of sustainability
> or interdependence, but by re-configuring how bodies inter-
> act with a world that threatens "to the skin," literary culture
> can help create new perspectives. The world in ecological
> crisis may not resemble a pastoral garden so much as the
> sea in flood.[64]

Mentz's analysis of how the shift in "the controlling metaphors"
from stability to disequilibrium "literalizes the crisis of the au-

---

62 "Low subject" is Patricia Fumerton's description of a "multiply displaced
   identity formation" representative of itinerant laborers through the songs
   and ballads of the period. "The unsettled subject," she explains, shifts "from
   place to place, relationship to relationship, and job to job," and is "'appren-
   ticed' in a range of different identities or roles without ever attaining the
   'freedom' of formulating an integrated and singular subjectivity" (Fumerton,
   Unsettled, 51).

63 Shakespeare may be seeing through the Reformation zeal that supports such
   laws.

64 Steve Mentz, "Strange Weather in *King Lear*," *Shakespeare* 6.2: 139–52; 146–
   47.

thority in the play" offers a powerful instance of the tragic genre's ability to invert the ideological energies of the theater, especially in the way the early modern stage often reconstituted the
social order through romantic conceptions of organic harmony.
Mentz's powerful analysis, in fact, allows for a critical retool-
ing of theater's ecological relation to what older theme critics
used to call the "natural order." We might build on Mentz's idea
of the storm as an agent that reassembles new ecological place-
ments by seeing the heath as the mirror opposite of the comedic
green world posited by Northrop Frye.[65] Rather than subject-
ing human relations to the scandal of folly and unpredictability
to "clarify" and "reconstitute" the character's place in the social
order, the destabilizing gray world of the heath positions characters to stare their thingness in the face, to see something like
the inert death of their being that Freud posited could be seen
in the *unheimliche* of the doll's eyes.[66] "First of difference and
decay," Kent says to acknowledge his identity among the slain
on a battlefield at the end of the play (5.3.287), revealing Shakespeare's vision of life's affirmation at the very point of its dissipation. If there is clarification here, it is not to restore any totem or
hierarchy, but to subject that hierarchy to a disturbing picture of
death-in-being, like a statue made of sand that will inevitably return to its particle existence, the human "sees itself" in its innate
thingness as object — the inanimate in the animate — subject to
the same forces of nature as everything else. Lear's famous dic-
tum "we came crying hither" is meant to voice the profound
bleakness of life's finitude. The inertness of death is symbol-

---

65 Northrop Frye, *Anatomy of Criticism* (Princeton: Princeton University
    Press, 1951), 182–84. Frye associated the heath in Shakespeare with the veg-
    etable world or the "sinister forest" (138).
66 Compare this idea of the gray world with Michael Ignatieff's idea of the heath
    as symbolizing the "vast gray space of state confinement." On the wards of
    psychiatric hospitals, the attendants shovel gruel into the mouths of vacant
    or unwilling patients; in the dispensaries, the drug trays are prepared; on the
    catwalks of the prisons, dinner is slopped into tin trays and thrust into cells.
    Needs are met, but souls are dishonoured. Natural man — the "poor, bare,
    forked animal" — is maintained; the social man wastes away (Ignatieff, *The
    Needs of Strangers*, 50–51).

ized in Lear's ironic command to Gloucester to "get thee glass eyes," to "seem / To see the things thou dost not" (4.6.65–66). Humans are objects to the unfeeling justice whose "glass eyes" cannot discern the difference in things: all accounted for equally against the same hollow background. The storm on the heath is antithetical to human nature, a zero-sum energy that, like the relational equivalence of any assemblage, translates it into an entity to be defined in its absence. Kent describes the storm as unknown, before memory, a kind of antipodal hell opposed to even "wanderers of the dark" (3.2.42).

> [T]hings that love night
> Love not such nights as these; the wrathful skies
> Gallow the very wanderers of the dark,
> And make them keep their caves: since I was man,
> Such sheets of fire, such bursts of horrid thunder,
> Such groans of roaring wind and rain, I never
> Remember to have heard: man's nature cannot carry
> The affliction nor the fear. (3.2.40–47)

Later, Lear tells Kent, "Thou think'st 'tis much that this contentious storm / Invades us to the skin." To you, maybe, he explains: "So 'tis to thee" (3.4.7–8). But not Lear. To explain how such a terrifying storm does not lay siege to his body, he uses the analogy:

> But where the greater malady is fix'd,
> The lesser is scarce felt. Thou'ldst shun a bear;
> But if thy flight lay toward the raging sea,
> Thou'ldst meet the bear i' the mouth. (3.4.9–12)

At this point "the tempest in [his] mind" is that which fixes Lear's resolve against the elements. The agony of his emotional turmoil is greater than the storm. One could use this passage to reassert the argument that Lear's subjective position conveys value or meaning to that which he experiences: his environment (existence), in a word, co-relates to his being, as the speculative realists might say. But this passage demonstrates the tangential, relational quality of new materialism's idea of agency. Lear complains too much, in a word, about his vulnerability. Lear's examples belong to the bare arts of the Phrygian elements: he means to instruct Kent on his inner anguish, but to do so he reveals his vital dependence on his environment to make the very point. Shunning a bear and avoiding fierce undertows are commonplace forms of wisdom foregrounded in his assertions. A philosophical reading of this passage dramatizes the inflexible nature of the web of determinations involved in the making of social catastrophe, where the instincts of fight or flight and avoiding tidal swells define Lear's humanity as one agent against others on the horizon.

The intensity of the gray space to reduce all objects to the same accounting according to a primeval scale of being finds its correlate in the science-fiction novel, Joe Haldeman's now classic *The Forever War*. Haldeman envisions the "stasis field," an imagined energy shield used by soldiers as a last resort that hovers over their heads, negating all atomic energy and preventing penetration from anything traveling faster than a manually-thrown projectile. The field cancels out the use of advanced weapons like deadly rays, nuclear warheads, and high velocity bullets or rockets that might rely on magnetic energy. If a rocket enters the field, it slows and drops to the ground like a rock.

> Nothing could move at greater than 16.3 meters per second inside the field, which was a hemispherical (in space, spherical) volume about fifty meters in radius. Inside, there was no such thing as electromagnetic radiation; no electricity, no magnetism, no light. From inside your suit, you could see surroundings in ghostly monochrome — which phenomenon was glibly explained to me as being due to "phase transference of quasi-energy leaking through from an adjacent tachyon reality," so much phlogiston to me.[67]

67 Joe Haldeman, *The Forever War* (New York: St Martin's, 1974), 204.

As a literary device the stasis field is a morbidly playful meta-phor with its roots in the jungle warfare Haldeman witnessed in Vietnam. Like the "magic portal" trope of the genre, which allows the author to transplant characters into any historical set-ting to illuminate the constructedness of their world views, this gadget effects the reverse. Here, the magic is to wipe away the very tropes of science fiction itself, to put the imaginative capac-ities of the genre to manufacture new technologies to conquer space travel and the unknown immensity of the galaxies on hold in order to bring us back to the reality of warfare. It is a technol-ogy that reverses technology, a kind of utopian first world wish fulfillment that other countries do not develop nuclear arma-ments. Importantly, at the level of characters, the stasis field also cancels every distinction so that all beings are reduced to some primitive state of existence. The stasis field is a kind of stripping down to the essential of all beings-things-objects to their inert core, an advanced piece of technology that enforces a return to a geological moment where survival means answering to the ba-sics of Newtonian physics. Used as a clever weapon, it forces all soldiers, regardless of how technologically advanced their soci-ety, to use spears, bows and arrows, and swords to fight hand-to-hand. Picked up and carried over any battlefield, it serves as a shield to megaton blasts dropped from above, but it also reduces all under it, regardless of technological superiority, to a brutally level playing field.

Shakespeare's heath, like an early modern version of the sta-sis field, forces a similar kind of flatness on its animate objects: instead of technological differences, think of the morphologi-cal differences between species as subject to a similar leveling pattern, a "phase transference" that blinds the human eyes to its privileged hierarchies — a medieval field that reduces every-thing to the same physical equation, all objects bound in time to fall to the ground like rocks. If the court symbolizes the po-tential overabundance of the Anthropocene, the heath can serve as a dim reminder of the shanty-town scarcity upon which its excess depends, highlighted in all its ghostly monochrome. The heath, then, could stand in as Shakespeare's version of what the new materialism calls "flat ontology." Echoing the term flat geometry and its related notion of affine space from mathematics, the idea of flat ontology for eco-materialists is meant to be the strongest possible argument against the phenomenological claim that the world's noumenal essence (thing in itself) is finally inflected by the human subject's relation to it. As described by Diana Coole and Samantha Frost, the new materialism works against the "Cartesian–Newtonian understanding of matter" which "portrays humans as rational, self-aware, free, and self-moving agents. Such subjects are not only deemed capable of making sense of nature by measuring and classifying it from a distance but are also aided in such a quest by theories whose application enables them to manipulate and reconfigure matter on an unprecedented scale."[68] Against this idea of what they term the "modern attitude or ethos of subjectivist potency," the new materialism posits a collective form of agency that includes not just "the human," but the "emergent, generative powers (or agenic capacities) even with inorganic matter."[69] The term "flat ontology" is attributed to Manuel DeLanda, who in his *Intensive Science and Virtual Philosophy* attempts to get at the "flux" of energies and agents involved in any form of socio-environmental change. He explains that a flat ontology is based

> on relations between general types and particular instances . . . each level representing a different ontological category (organism, species, genera), an approach in terms of interacting parts and emergent wholes leads to a flat ontology, one made exclusively of unique, singular individuals, differing in spatio-temporal scale but not in ontological status.[70]

68 Diana Coole and Samantha Frost, ed., *New Materialisms: Ontology, Agency, and Politics* (Durham: Duke University Press, 2010), 8.

69 Ibid., 9.

70 Manuel DeLanda, *Intensive Science and Virtual Philosophy* (London: Continuum Press, 2005), 58.

As a general concept that means to move away from hierarchical models of historical change, the roots of the idea of a more "embedded" or "multi-causal" model can be traced through Gilles Deleuze's idea of individuation and Bruno Latour's philosophy of scientific realism.[71] New materialism's investment in the flat ontology means to expose what is sometimes described as the "immanent" effect of the generative powers of the relational sum of interactive organic and inorganic entities. In his *Pandora's Hope,* Bruno Latour imagines a collective host of actions behind each event that are involved in the "becoming" (his term, "becoming collective"), a new understanding of human motivation that is caught in a web of layered causes and effects. He describes this endlessly receding line of causality as a "technical delegation" of causes that bears down upon and becomes an equal player in any human action. He offers the famous example of the speed bump that slows the driver, who slows down not out of a moral sense of safety for others but to keep his car from being damaged. Slow drivers because concern for others? Or slow drivers because concern for car? The "effect" of slowing is the same: slower drivers on the road. But the driver's motivations (that of the Subject by analogy) are now bracketed as nearly inconsequential to the effect. The Subject's role in the slowing is de-emphasized, a small piece of the larger picture. Latour imagines a coming together of gravity, tarmac, city zoning committees, neighborhood watch groups, the particular physics of automobile suspension, and the driver's anticipation of the thump, the pressing of the brake pedal, the tightening of the coil spring, the car's shifting of counter weight to allow for the tire to now lift into the well without maxing the shock ... *ad infinitum,* all come into play and have equal part in the "effect" — but also the feel, the experience — of the slowing. Latour works through the metaphor of "shifting down" (now the historian and not the driver), "that crosses over with entities that have a different tim-

71 Gilles Deleuze, *Difference and Repetition,* trans. Paul Patton (London: Athlone Press, 1997); Bruno Latour, *Pandora's Hope: Essays on the Reality of Science Studies* (Cambridge: Harvard University Press, 1999).

ing, different spaces, different properties, different ontologies, and that are made to share the same destiny, thus creating a new actant."[72] As such, the idea of a flat ontology works much like Haldeman's metaphor of the stasis field, except in terms of an animal-object's place in a non-hierarchical "transference" of relationality, where humans and things are now related according to a more advanced grid of energy, causes, and effects, where a system of air-water-earth-energy work to place all things in a multiple causality of "linked" material objectifications. "For materiality is always something more than 'mere' matter," Coole and Frost explain, it is

> an excess, force, vitality, relationality, or difference that renders matter active, self-creative, productive, unpredictable … evincing immanent modes of self-transformation that compel us to think of causation in far more complex terms [as] phenomena … caught in a multitude of interlocking systems.[73]

Forked Animals

> Mr. William Shakespeare was born at Stratford-upon-Avon, in the county Warwick. His father was a butcher, and I have been told heretofore by some of his neighbors that, when he was a boy, he exercised his father's trade; but when he killed a calfe he would doe it in the high style and make a speech.
> — John Aubrey, *Brief Lives*[74]

One of the legends surrounding Shakespeare's otherwise notoriously sparse archival presence in the records of his time is that,

---

72 Latour, *Pandora's Hope,* 192.

73 Coole and Frost, *New Materialisms,* 9.

74 John Aubrey, *Brief Lives* (Woodbridge: Boydell, 1982), 285. But there is always a grain of truth in Aubrey's reports: to this day, tourists are told that behind John Shakespeare's house there stood for years buildings used as a tannery, to butcher animals and tan their hides.

as the son of a "tanner," he may have been called upon to help butcher animals to process the leather. We know that Shakespeare's father was a wittawer, a maker of gloves and leather goods, and not, as Aubrey reports, a butcher. John Shakespeare was a maker of what today we call "luxury goods," fine leather goods which he made and sold out of his house on Henley Street, Stratford. I am intrigued by Michael Wood's argument about how John Shakespeare's illegal side-trade as a freelance "brogger," someone who illegally sold wool because he was not licensed, underscores Shakespeare's awareness of the wool trade in many plays.[75] A tanner who tans leather, including sheepskin, may have had at times bundles of fleece to sell illegally, or throw away. But awareness of this ironic logic of throwing away useful goods (to stay within the law) in order to produce other valuable items can be seen in *Lear*. The core logic of the Anthropocene today, regrettably, is the waste that is written into the very production quota of arable crops.[76] Shakespeare is exposed to the logic of excess through this trade: its place in the growing textile economy where sheep and the fencing of arable land through enclosures make the lives of Poor Tom less a fiction.[77] We are given a wonderful account of the destruction built into the production of profit within the Anthropocene in Hythloday's critique of the textile industry in Sir Thomas More's *Utopia*. If we were looking for a way to hypothesize the enmeshed existence behind *King Lear*'s heath, and how this connects to the aristocracy's investments to maintain their culture of prodigality, and how this in turn relates to sheepfolds and Poor Tom's diet, I can think of no better analysis than Hythloday's description of how the English sheep eat humans in More's *Utopia*. Here is a

---

75 Michael Wood, *Shakespeare* (New York: Basic Books, 2003), 42–43.

76 "Some 40% of food is thrown away in the rich world," Gaia Vince reminds us. "Cutting waste would be the fastest and cheapest way of meeting future global food requirements. Food wastage is the third largest emitter of greenhouse gases after US and China, and uses a third of agricultural land even though 870 million people go hungry every day" (Vince, *Adventures in the Anthropocene*, 144).

77 See Wood, *Shakespeare*, 42–43.

description of a fixed causality that links men with things and ecosystems: diet, health of species, production of corn and its sundry things, the effect of arable agriculture on humans, sheep, frogs, toads, tadpoles, wall-newts … and dead rats as food. The question for More is, "what causes crime?" But this quickly becomes an eco-materialist account of the waste predicated by the profligacy of the courteous classes:

> ["]Yet this is not the only force driving men to thievery. There is another that, as I see it, applies more specially to you Englishmen."
>
> "What is that?" said the Cardinal.
>
> "Your sheep," I said, "that commonly are so meek and eat so little; now, as I hear, they have become so greedy and fierce that they devour human beings themselves. They devastate and depopulate fields, houses, and towns. For in whatever parts of the land sheep yield the finest and thus the most expensive wool, there the nobility and gentry, yes, and even a good many abbots — holy men — are not content with the old rents that the land yielded to their predecessors. Living in idleness and luxury without doing society any good no longer satisfies them; they have to do positive harm. For they leave no land free for the plough; they enclose every acre for pasture; they destroy houses and abolish towns, keeping the churches — but only for sheep-barns. And as if enough of your land were not already wasted on game-preserves and forests for hunting wild animals, these worthy men turn all human habitations and cultivated fields back to wilderness. Thus, so that one greedy, insatiable glutton, a frightful plague to his native country, may enclose thousands of acres within a single fence, the tenants are ejected; and some are stripped of their belongings by trickery or brute force, or, wearied by constant harassment, are driven to sell them. One way or another, these wretched

people — men, women, husbands, wives, orphans, widows, parents with little children and entire families (poor but numerous, since farming requires many hands) — are forced to move out. They leave the only homes familiar to them, and can find no place to go. Since they must leave at once without waiting for a proper buyer, they sell for a pittance all their household goods, which would not bring much in any case. When that little money is gone (and it's soon spent in wandering from place to place), what finally remains for them but to steal, and so be hanged — justly, no doubt — or to wander and beg? And yet if they go tramping, they are jailed as idle vagrants. They would be glad to work, but they can find no one who will hire them. There is no need for farm labour, in which they have been trained, when there is no land left to be planted. One herdsman or shepherd can look after a flock of beasts large enough to stock an area that used to require many hands to make it grow crops.["] [78]

Shakespeare's tragedy is written decades after More's critique, but his vision of *King Lear*'s trek through the sheepfolds and the green mantle runoff can be seen to provide one of the most vivid artistic representations of a land denuded by disastrous legal ineptitude and economic abuse.[79] No side-glance is called for: this

78 Thomas More, *Utopia,* ed. George Logan and Robert Adams (Cambridge: Cambridge University Press, 1975), 18.

79 See Karen Raber's eco-material analysis of More's use of sheep in *Utopia* to unfound the notions of property in *Animal Bodies, Renaissance Culture* (Philadelphia: University of Pennsylvania Press, 2013). "By enforcing a system of global labor that inevitably also challenges distinctions between species on the basis of the work they do," she argues, "More's work also highlights the flaws in economic systems that create false differences between kinds of labor and/or laboring identities" (178). Also instructive is her assessment of the sheep conversation (my phrase) between critics who want to show Renaissance writers working against the grain of the Enlightenment human-animal binary by mobilizing images of sheep as metaphors for social displacement or philosophical idealism (162–63). Like Marx, these critics tend to replace actual material sheep for principled categories important to their own approach. See Paul A. Yachnin, "Sheepishness in The Winter's Tale," in *How to Do Things with Shakespeare*, ed. Laurie Maguire (Oxford and

entangled web of animal–man relationality underscores rural existence in the period. The idea of tragic "fate," that past actions are intricately caught up in an unfolding set of actions outside of our control, is the perfect genre for depicting the enmeshed causality of individual action, in this case England's rise to fame as the world's most powerful textile producer and how this is linked to the irony of Lear's journey from extravagant court to the vagrant's hovel. Shakespeare's representation of predatory man can be read to echo More's image of the heath.

Scholars since Raymond Williams have called for a revision of pastoral idealism underscored with the narrative of modernity.[80] It does not take much to push off-center this analysis to repurpose the older materialist critique to one that reveals the ecological theme of its central concern with sustainability. As modern readers, if we harbored any pastoral claim to this space as blissful, or innocent, or a retreat from the strife of the court, we are grimly reminded that it is in fact an agricultural war zone, where waste, crisis, and the resulting dehumanizing treatment of the poor are part of the legacy one witnesses when innocently reading sheep or thinking of "sheepcotes." There is a longstanding critical tradition that charts *King Lear's* use of animal imagery to depict the bestial and predatory instincts of man.[81] Where More saw idleness and pride at work in the

Malden, MA: Blackwell Publishing, 2008), 210–29. See also Julian Yates, "Humanist Habitats, or 'Eating Well' with Thomas More's *Utopia*," in *Environment and Embodiment in Early Modern England,* ed. Mary Floyd Wilson and Garrett A. Sullivan, Jr. (New York: Palgrave, 2007), 187–209; and "Counting Sheep: Dolly Does Utopia (again)," *Rhizomes* 8 (Spring 2004): http://www.rhizomes.net/issue8/yates2.htm.

80 Raymond Williams, *The Country and the City* (London: Chatto and Windus, 1973).

81 A.C. Bradley observes "the incessant references to the lower animals and man's likeness to them. These references are scattered broadcast through the whole play, as though Shakespeare's mind were so busy with the subject that he could hardly write a page without some allusion to it" (*Shakespearean Tragedy*, 266). See also George Coffin Taylor, "Shakespeare's Use of the Idea of the Beast in Man," in *Studies in Philology* 42.3 (1945): 530–43; John McCloskey, "The Emotive Use of Animal Imagery in *King Lear*," *Shakespeare Quarterly* 13.3 (1962): 321–25; and Alan Dent, *World of Shakespeare: Animals*

wealthy noblemen's rush to do "positive harm," as Hythloday terms it, Shakespeare gives us a human image of self-consuming depravity. Shakespeare has Lear recognizing "judicious punishment" in the image of his own offspring, Goneril and Regan, zombie-like, "consuming" him. When seeing Poor Tom (Edgar), he imagines that his own ungrateful daughters must be responsible for man's plight: "Is it the fashion that discarded fathers / Should have thus little mercy on their flesh?" (3.4.69–70). Lear depicts this in the Renaissance myth of pelicans that raise their young on their own blood. He concludes: "'t was this flesh begot those pelican daughters" (3.4.71). This theme is amplified later by Gloucester, who says, in proverbial reflection, "Our flesh and blood is grown so vile, my lord, / That it doth hate what gets it" (3.4.133–34). The theme of cosmic decay is elsewhere rearticulated as a central philosophical preoccupation of the tragedy, abstracted into a metaphysical process, informing its poetic rendering of a natural world torn from within. "Crack nature's molds, all germens spill at once" (3.2.8), Lear tells us, reiterating a Renaissance theme of mutability and nature's innate tendency to spill out of its prescribed limit. If there is immanence here, it is associated with a fallen world, internally putrescent, ruined pieces of nature, where things are enmeshed in a "ripeness" that signals an abundance of moldered waste. "Thou knowest, the first time that we smelled the air, / We wail and cry" (4.6.173–74).

When applied to the idea of insubordinate daughters and bastard sons, the image of decay is articulated through images of

& *Monsters* (New York: Taplinger, 1972). Recent scholarship looks with an ecological, post-Linnaean sensitive to the Renaissance fascination with the human-animal divide as it is constructed, questioned, and challenged in early modern writing. See Bruce Boeher's *Shakespeare Among the Animals: Nature and Society in the Drama of Early Modern England* (Basingstoke: Palgrave Macmillan, 2002) for an analysis of the animal metaphor as a mediation of the natural order composed in early modern drama. See also Erica Fudge's *Perceiving Animals: Humans and Beasts in Early Modern English Culture* (Urbana and Chicago: University of Illinois Press, 2002), and Erica Fudge, Ruth Gilbert, and Susan Wiseman, ed., *At the Borders of the Human: Beasts, Bodies, and Natural Philosophy in the Early Modern Period* (Basingstoke: Palgrave Macmillan, 1999).

predatory depravity. The imagery resonates with Christian–Dionysian traces of immolation and consumption. Scholars point to the earlier *King Leir* (1605) again to find the primal scene of influence on Shakespeare's use of recurring images of cannibalism to depict human violence.[82] In *Leir*, it is often pointed out, the "trigger" for these images of self-consuming flesh is an even more frightening image of omaphagic sacrifice. At their lowest point on their journey to France, the Kent character, Perillus, begs to feed his king with his very blood:

> PERILLUS: Ah, my dear Lord, how doth my heart lament,…
> To see you brought to this extremity!
> O, if you love me, as you do profess,
> Or ever thought well of me in my life, [He strips up his arms.]
> Feed on this flesh, whose veins are not so dry,
> But there is virtue left to comfort you.
> O, feed on this, if this will do you good,
> I'll smile for joy, to see you suck my blood.
> LEIR: I am no Cannibal, that I should delight
> To slake my hungry jaws with human flesh:
> I am no devil, or ten times worse than so,…
> To suck the blood of such a peerless friend.
> O, do not think that I respect my life
> So dearly, as I do thy loyal love.
> Ah, Britain, I shall never see thee more,
> That hast unkindly banished thy King:
> And yet thou dost not make me to complain,

---

82 For the historical context of cannibalism in the English early modern imaginary, see Bernard Sheehan, *Savagism and Civility: Indians and Englishmen in Colonial Virginia* (Cambridge: Cambridge University Press, 1980); Peter Hulme, *Colonial Encounters: Europe and the Native Caribbean, 1492–1797* (London: Routledge, 1987). For the relation to "Sythian" in *Lear*, see Derek Hirst's "Text, time, and the pursuit of 'British identities,'" in *British Identities and English Renaissance Literature,* ed. David Baker and Willy Maley (Cambridge: Cambridge University Press, 2002), 256–66.

But they which were more near to me than thou.[83]

It might be worth pausing to consider what the original *Leir* depicts in this scene, and why, perhaps, it is so hauntingly familiar to those who have read Shakespeare's tragedy. The King argues that he is above cannibalism, that he will not "slake [his] hungry jaws with human flesh," but the imagery is *unheimliche* precisely because it reminds the audience of the predatory relations that subtend the official courtly relations of the king. Perillus offers his blood to suck to a dying king, now put in a grim, unholy position of child to the knight's Madonna, an image of a juvenilized king that may have inspired Shakespeare's version in his Fool's taunt to Lear, "ever since thou madest thy daughters thy mothers. For when thou gavest them the rod, and put'st down thine own breeches" (1.4.149–51). Perillus offers his lifeblood as the ultimate symbol of duty. In keeping with a visual pun, the scene puts into striking image the idea of the king's needs draining the vassal of his service and provisions, a kind of literalization of aristocratic expenditure sucking dry even his manor hosts on his progress, depicting the self-sacrifice implicit in "service" as one of the only "virtue[s] left to comfort" the king. Shakespeare switches the tenor of this image of sacrifice and scarcity, revising it into a misogynist fantasy of unfaithful "Pelican daughters" preying on the patriarch, who is now a victim to his children's cannibalistic cravings. The revision works to emphasize the economy of expenditure that sits at the center of the second half of the play's focus on the heath. Lear's famous epiphany on the heath underscores this aspect of his identity. The "unaccommodated man" speech is meant to voice a kind of early modern version of "natural man," the idealized image of a person shorn from social contexts and thus clarified to a bare essence. He sees Edgar as Poor Tom through the "phase transference" that is the Renaissance stasis field, which now makes all humans radically

83 *King Leir,* "Precursors of Shakespeare Plays," at *Elizabethan Authors,* transcribed by Barboura Flues, ed. Robert Brazil, http://www.elizabethanauthors.org/king-leir-1605-1-16.htm, 24.30–47.

equivalent in the thorny way, say, of seeing the crude inanimate randomness of our forked body for the first time in one's crooked toenails or the caked skin crimped over our bony digits and being shocked with its shuddersome organic otherness.[84] Lear responds:

Why, thou wert better in thy grave than to answer
with thy uncovered body this extremity of the skies.
Is man no more than this? Consider him well. Thou
owest the worm no silk, the beast no hide, the sheep
no wool, the cat no perfume. Ha! here's three on
's are sophisticated! Thou art the thing itself:
unaccommodated man is no more but such a poor, bare,
forked animal as thou art. Off, off, you lendings!
come unbutton here. (3.4.94–101)

---

84 I am indebted to Laurie Shannon's *The Accomodated Animal: Cosmopolity in Shakespearean Locales* (Chicago: University of Chicago Press, 2013), especially her discussion of the "zoographic" discourse in the play, a mode of comparison of human and beasts "that evaluates an integrity in beasts that it asserts man lacks" (140). The terms of her analysis allow her to flesh out a more complicated human-animal relation than is usually asserted in assessments of the neoplatonic views of the human as elevated above or outside the animal kingdom. The valuation of animals as keenly endowed with special talents or prowess she terms "human negative exceptionalism." See especially her analysis in Chapter Three, "Poor, Bare, Forked: Animal Happiness and the Zoographic Critique of Humanity," of the Renaissance "body inventories" of hides and hair that endow animals with special adaptive capacities. "*King Lear* relentlessly voices the grim reckoning of human estate that was forged in the happy beast tradition," she argues. "The play's persistent absorption with unclad bodies and unkind relations raises a transhistorical problem in philosophy and theology — humankind's cosmic place — but its mode of inquiry and its answers express a zoographic critique of man, all the way down" (165). My emphasis is on Shakespeare's place in the production of luxury goods — itself a symptom of aristocratic prodigality — a trade in which his family prospered. To assert the hides and gowns work in a larger economy responsible for the heath and its destabilizing force is to say that "negative exceptionalism" is a product of early modern social rituals, and not so much a philosophical (ontological) condition.

Lear cannot keep from referencing the animal residue that clings to the objects we use to clothe our bodies: worms, civets, and sheep are related only in that they also produce the inanimate objects used to maintain our social identity and assert hierarchical status. Shakespeare's father's trade produced precisely those kinds of luxurious status symbols that are a "superflux" on the heath. This wish to distinguish oneself through the "effects of courtesy" by wearing fine garments and perfume resonates through Lear's citational reflection.

Let us return to the image of a young Shakespeare helping his father (or his father's partner) slaughter sheep or calves for napa leather gloves or a fur cloak.[85] Let us imagine that Aubrey overheard something of a half truth in this rumor of a family with several children pressed into the labor of butchering live rabbits, minks, or ermine "in a high style" to aid in a family business. Is it that difficult to see a child uttering memorized words — not tragic lines but something else maybe from the book of Proverbs — under his breath as the dead animal loosens its bowels in death on his shoes? As the steam rises from the warm feces and blood, what kind of thoughts might a young man have about himself? His place? His possibilities? We can only imagine how this kind of work would mark a child, especially someone endowed with the capability to see through the eyes of others. A young man's conscience could not help but be held in an inescapable sense of the frailty of life measured by the difference between humans and animals. Returning to family and com-

85 See Katherine Duncan-Jones's *Shakespeare: Upstart Crow to Sweet Swan, 1592–1623* (London: Methuen Drama, 2011), especially her tracing of the related material to Aubrey's account of Shakespeare's high style as butcher in her chapter "Kill Cow" (1–26). Though there were explicit prohibitions against whittawers butchering their own animals, Aubrey's report on this rumor is — like all of the archival reports — teasingly graphic in what it says about the possible contexts of the poet's upbringing. John Shakespeare was friends and partners with William Tyler, a butcher by trade. "Shakespeare and his siblings may have helped with animals skins at an early age in their father's workshop. The games they played at home may have been influenced both by real-life spectacle of animals being killed in Stratford slaughterhouses" (15).

munity, and to the small market town, would mean returning to this scene at his father's tannery behind Henley Street. Thoughts of leaving and returning would take on such profoundly contradictory feelings of obligation, waste, and debt.

In the above passage about "sophisticated" humans, Lear uses a perfect paradox about the benefit of being debt-free, expressing in proverbial form how the naked and destitute are advantaged by their lack: "Thou owest the worm no silk, the beast no hide, the sheep no wool." But they are debt-free only in the sense that humans owe to other animals their very existence. How does Lear return the lent clothing? And to whom? "Come unbutton here." These clothes and status symbols are made shadows by the ontic decentering of the heath. Edgar's disguise as naked bedlam triggers a self-recognition: Lear's reminded that his entire entourage — the Fool, Kent and Gloucester — are as "sophisticated" as the naked man before them. The heath's poetic effect is to remind Lear of his (in)animate self and to reflect on precisely that buried or repressed truth that motivated his love test at the beginning of the story: his dependence on others. The real tragedy of the play is whether Lear will accept his relational dependence as one forked animal among others in his environment, whether he will read agency or affect through the grid of a flat ontology. Forked animals, all, as we hear the thud of his "lendings" — for they are now strangely not his, just borrowed skin to assert an imagined privilege — loft in the wind before hitting the dirt.

Lear's Receding World

The spider says to the centipede, "Look here, I have only eight legs. I can manage eight, but you have a hundred. I cannot imagine how it is that you know at each moment which of your hundred legs to move." So the centipede said, "It is very simple." And he has been paralyzed ever since. Now the centipede effect is a very real effect. The violinist Adolph Busch — perhaps some of you know his name — he told me once that he played Beethoven's Violin Concerto in Zurich, and afterwards the violinist Huberman came and asked him how he played a certain passage. Busch said it was quite simple — and then found that he could no longer play the passage. The attempt to do it consciously interfered with his fingering, or whatever it was, and he could no longer do it. That is very interesting and actually shows the function of this process of becoming unconscious.

— Karl Popper, *Knowledge and the Body–Mind Problem*[1]

Mnemonic Speech as Human Automata

In an aside, Curtis Perry suggests in his *Making of Jacobean Culture* that "Lear's invective against his pelican daughters expresses, in a remarkably condensed form, the perception that the cornucopian rhetoric of the play's first scene was misleading."[2]

1   Karl Popper, *Knowledge and the Body–Mind Problem: In Defense of Interaction,* ed. M.A. Notturno (London: Routledge, 1994), 116.

2   Curtis Perry, *The Making of Jacobean Culture: James I and the Renegotiation of Elizabethan Literary Practice* (Cambridge: Cambridge University Press,

"Lear discovers," Perry continues, "that his is a world of scarcity, a world in which bounty cannot be bottomless, and in which resources must be husbanded with care."[3] Perry's suggestive terms, "scarcity," "resources," "husband," work to promote a formalist sense of balance in the play's investigation of morality. I want to build on Perry's assertion that the world of scarcity occasions a different management of inwardness. His claims can also work to surmise how the ecological shift to the mechanical tone in the end of the play belongs not just to a different linguistic economy but to a thing world where humans coexist with animals and natural forces. As I have argued, the move from court to heath activates a different sense of language as tool-being: from that of masking intent, participating in the flourish of aristocratic prodigality and circumstance, to that of survival and pondering one's relation in the interdependence of a denuded world. Following the lead of other eco-materialists and their readings of Shakespeare's posthuman strains, including Steve Mentz, Karen Raber, Julian Yates, and others, I have framed the thematic arc of Shakespeare's tragedy about the fall of a king as a tableaux of our post-sustainable condition, as we move from one of supposed luxury and boundless resources, to the naked accommodations of the Anthropocene.[4] Lear's progress on the heath works as a

1997), 133.

3   Ibid.

4   See Julian Yates, *Error, Misuse, Failure: Object Lessons From The English Renaissance* (Minneapolis: University of Minnesota Press, 2003). See also Julian Yates, "Shakespeare's Kitchen Archives," in *Speculative Medievalisms: Discography,* ed. Petropunk Collective [Eileen Joy, Anna Klosowska, Nicola Masciandaro, and Michael O'Rourke] (Brooklyn: punctum books, 2013), 179–200; and "Accidental Shakespeare," *Shakespeare Studies* 34 (2006): 90–122. Steve Mentz's latest work to uncover what he has called the "proto-ecological system" in early modern representations of the sea, ocean travel, and storms presents the strongest model yet of adapting historicism to an ecological-minded criticism. See Steve Mentz, *At the Bottom of Shakespeare's Ocean* (London: Continuum, 2009). Andy Mousely examines the continuities between skepticism and posthumanist ethics in "Care, Scepticism and Speaking in the Plural: Posthumanisms and Humanisms in *King Lear*" in *Posthumanist Shakespeares,* ed. Stefan Herbrechter and Ivan Callus (London: Palgrave, 2012), 97–113.

parable of flat ontology. But Lear's story offers another cautionary fable about abdicating sovereignty in our very thinking of
agency. Lear moves from subject to object. That we are caught
in a multitude of interlocking systems echoes a tragic theme of
battling against forces beyond our control. His status is desanc-
tified by the gray world, as he is made to realize he is one agent
among many in nature's elements. Such a reimagining of this
tragedy is important because it asks that we place its central existential questions (the meaning of familial love, commitments
to friends, our place in a secular world) in a new relation to the
main question of surviving within fixed environmental limits.
For if we cannot manage to maintain a sustainable environment,
these other questions that motor much of the humanities will
eventually become superfluous intellectual commitments.

Here in this coda I want to tie together the threads of my
reading: *King Lear*'s skeptical reflections on faith, proverbial
speech, and its occurrence in the gray world. We are in a position to theorize how mnemonic reflection functions as a potentially empowering mode of consciousness that is responding
to its environment. Not seen as inducing a somnambulant state
or unselfconscious awareness, but a mode of fragmentary, vital
representation whose process brings us closer to our lived environment as animals in relation to our existence, providing a
side-glance of our world not adequately witnessed or rendered
in narrative. In this instance, proverbial speech can be considered a mode of speech that counteracts the lived environment of
courtly opulence and prodigality, the world of rhetorical display
and the superflux of language, by bringing us back to the thing-
existence of an imagined past.

As we have been discussing in the past chapters, *King Lear*
holds out for the "return" of one element of this lost world. The
play clings to the ritualized shell of the animatronic practices
implicit in humanist modes of memory work. One objection
to my argument might be that I am trying to recuperate unconscious or intuitive modes of awareness as sites of resistance.
There is a strong current of historical scholarship that traces the
critique by Reformation thinkers of church ceremony ritual as

mechanical, hence a form of hallucination and witchcraft. This is to say that the sixteenth century develops a rather nuanced set of terms to recognize the ideological — faith as false consciousness. Following Keith Thomas's monumental *Religion and the Decline of Magic,* there is a series of revisionist historicism that focuses on precisely this critique of ceremony as theater and hence as a primary semiotext for understanding the secular strains of modern English theater.[5] Much of this criticism is aimed at positioning the early modern playhouse as a secular space that, like Brecht's modernist drama, uses distancing techniques to unhinge or distort religious practice as a false belief system. I have no doubt that much of *King Lear* is aimed at precisely this form of self-awareness. On a deeper level, it is true, the play's interrogation of its privileged term, primogeniture, is subtle and corrosive. Though it could be said to reconstitute our belief in primogeniture in the Gloucester–Edgar plot, it seems consciously to counter this ideal in its view of Lear's eldest daughters (it is Cordelia, the youngest, who seems to deserve the full attention of inheritance). Also, too, as discussed by Stanley Cavell, Edmund's complaint against primogeniture, though

5   Keith Thomas, *Religion and the Decline of Magic* (London: Penguin, 2013). The critical conversation about theater as a medium that estranges religious practices can be traced in the feminist historicism's original focus on the representation of gender in antitheatrical tracts. See Jean Howard, "Renaissance Antitheatricality and the Politics of Gender and Rank in *Much Ado About Nothing*," in *Shakespeare Reproduced: Text and History in Ideology,* ed. Jean Howard and Marion F. O'Connor (New York: Methuen, 1987). But see also Lisa Freeman, "Jeremy Collier and the Politics of Theatrical Representation," in *Players, Playwrights, Playhouses: Investigating Performance, 1660–1800,* ed. Michael Cordner and Peter Holland (Basingstoke, England: Palgrave Macmillan, 2007), 135–51; Jean Marsden, "Female Spectatorship, Jeremy Collier and the Anti-Theatrical Debate," *ELH* 65 (1998): 877–98. Particularly as the distancing of ritual is represented in the tracts, and as it relates to *King Lear,* see Stephen Greenblatt's "Shakespeare and the Exorcists," in *Shakespearean Negotiations: The Circulation of Social Energy in Renaissance England* (Berkeley: University of California Press, 1988). See also Kevin Berland, "Bribing Aristophanes: The Uses of History and the Attack on the Theater in England," in *Sustaining Literature: Essays on Literature, History, and Culture, 1500–1800,* ed. Greg Clingham (Lewisburg, PA: Bucknell University Press, 2007), 229–46.

overtly challenged in its representation of him as a Machiavellian class climber, seems nonetheless logically consistent and sympathetically drawn. The play seems genuinely interested in the question why, exactly, people like Gloucester will not let sons born out of wedlock inherit property. Cavell suggests:

> In that soliloquy Edmund rails equally against his treatment as a bastard and as a younger son — as if to ask why a younger son should be treated like a bastard. Both social institutions seem to him arbitrary and unnatural. And nothing in the play shows him to be wrong, certainly not the behavior of Lear's legitimate older daughters, nor of Regan's lawful husband, nor of legitimate King Lear, who goes through an abdication without abdicating, and whose last legitimate act is to banish love and service from his realm. When Shakespeare writes a revenge tragedy, it is *Hamlet*; and when he presents us with a Bastard, legitimacy as a whole is thrown into question.[6]

The entire play stages moments of such discoveries precisely as keen moments of unveiling: Gloucester does indeed learn of his treatment of his son as a kind of shock to his senses — "O my follies! Then Edgar was abused. / Kind Gods, forgive me that, and prosper him!" (3.7.90–1). Lear must "see" his treatment in a similar way, too late perhaps, but in the full light of day. The fact that these characters become "whole," in the older formalist meaning of the term, as people, is open to interpretation. It's another question altogether whether this form of self-awareness instills in them any more agency to change the direction of their unfolding life.

I am not arguing that we jettison the idea of literature's capacity to critique ideology. My emphasis on the return to proverbial speech as an inward shift to mnemonic modes of awareness

6   Stanley Cavell, "The Avoidance of Love: A Reading of *King Lear*," in *Disowning Knowledge in Seven Plays of Shakespeare* (Cambridge: Cambridge University Press, 2003), 49.

should be set against the deeper cynicism of the play, because even if the tragedy depicts scenes of self-discovery, it does not effectively endorse these moments of revelation as empowering. Again, perhaps Cavell's sensitive philosophical rendering of the tragedy summarizes best the skepticism of the play when he says that tragedy as a genre is outworn in our world. "That one has to die in order to become reborn is one tragic fact," he explains.

> That one's wholeness deprives others of their life is another; that one's love becomes incompatible with one's life and kills the thing it loves is another. Lear is reborn, but into his old self. That is no longer just tragic, it suggests that tragedy itself has become ineffective, out-worn, because now even death does not overcome our difference. Here again, Gloucester's life amplifies Lear's. For it is one thing, and tragic, that we can learn only through suffering. It is something else that we have nothing to learn from it.[7]

If we inherit tragedy, like we have inherited other psychological mechanisms, as a moral grammar that no longer obtains to our present environment, we need to rethink how we can repurpose its skeptical vision of the world, how we can accessorize it for the Anthropocene. Cavell suggests the tragedy's aesthetic distancing does not hold hope for any kind of agential self-awareness. Perhaps we can return to the idea of textual dissonance and see how it is rendered. I would like to suggest the moment of the Anthropocene as the backdrop for the tragedy's staged retreat to mnemonic modes of representation. If the Anthropocene requires that we rethink not just sustainable practices and what Joanna Zylinska calls "minimal ethics," it also suggests that we rethink the value of literature as a tool to return to the bare arts of lost pedagogical practices, to a posthuman paramiology.[8] Literary narrative should be part of our toolkit for

---

7 Ibid., 340.
8 Joanna Zylinska, *Minimal Ethics for the Anthropocene* (Ann Arbor: Open Humanities Press/MPublishing, 2014).

the sustainable future. From a structuralist perspective, the "value" of the linguistic sign can carry within it a range of affective responses and emotional intensities, but the tools to read these postures seem woefully inadequate to the task of charting from where or whence they become intelligible as a text. Rather, the eco-materialist attention to the body as "enmeshed" by its own macro- and micro-object world (from the organisms in and out of its parasitical gastro-fauna, its DNA, and its vital chemical reactions and psychosomatic affectual spectrum), as well as the body as its own "object" in a flat ontology of cause and effect, asks us to attend to the possibility that memory, at least as it is passed down through the proverb from generation to generation, is something that is part of our disembodied posthuman past, something that was internalized as a species. That is, we might want to begin seeing memory as a trans-subjective experience, as something we can inherit as an evolutionary response to crisis and catastrophe. It is worth remembering the ancient roots of tragedy, too, in the rituals of social purification and exorcism. To ask the question about mnemonic modes of human creativity is to restore to the play its proverbial status as "catalyst" of self-invention. I believe *King Lear* is one of the greatest experiments in humanist literacy, a wildly self-reflexive and profoundly probing work of art aimed at dislocating the power of state and church. When the dust settles, the characters are so alienated from their earlier faith as to be left only with the outer shell of its rituals, a forced pharisaical skepticism, where rote language is offered as a solution to the narrative's vision of social dissolution.

As I have suggested in this book, I think the play offers its own allegory about the consequences of abdicating sovereignty in our own theoretical turns to object-oriented interpretations. *King Lear*'s positing of this supernatural force and the power it exerts on the thing world of the play can be read as a parable of the Heideggerian notion of the receding object. Ian Bogost has explained this decentering as a critical act that forces a new perception of our place in the world: "If we take seriously the idea that all objects recede interminably into themselves," he explains, "then human perception becomes just one among many ways that objects might relate. To put things at the center of a new metaphysics also requires us to admit that they do not exist just for us."[9] One of the seismic epiphanies of *King Lear* is when the king realizes he is in a world not centered around his sovereign existence, an "O without a figure" (1.4.168). On the surface, admittedly, it is not much of a feat to argue that Shakespeare's tragedy is reflecting in its own terms on the same questions of ontology that motor the new realism. The difference is that, for Shakespeare, there is a pathos to the awareness that human subjectivity is not endowed with a privileged place to escape the cosmic forces that lead to entropy with the world. In the theory of object-oriented philosophy like that promoted by some eco-materialists, however, there is a value to the knowledge that our being is one with the radical democracy of objects, not so much a mordant awareness of apocalypse but a finer understanding of our chances at surviving as a species if we work toward a sustainable future.

In the realm of science known as evolutionary psychology, there is an awareness of the belated nature of what is called, simply, "psychological mechanisms," behaviors that have come to define our instincts as a species to survive within specific environments. In their *Sense and Nonsense: Evolutionary Perspectives on Human Behavior,* Kevin Laland and Gillian Brown define these behaviors "broadly to include context-specific emotions, preferences, and proclivities [that] recurrently solved a specific problem of survival or reproduction over evolutionary history."[10] The list of such behaviors include basic drives and emotions like "jealousy ... fear of snakes and spiders, a preference for savannah landscapes, a capacity to learn a spoken language, preferences for particular characteristics in a partner, and a sensitivity to cheating."[11] The emphasis in evolutionary

9   Ian Bogost, *Alien Phenomenology, or What It's Like To Be A Thing* (Minneapolis: Minnesota University Press, 2012), 9.

10 Kevin Laland and Gillian Brown, *Sense and Nonsense: Evolutionary Perspectives on Human Behavior* (Oxford: Oxford University Press, 2002), 158.

11 Ibid., 157.

psychology is on the belated nature of culture, how some of our most basic drives and instincts as a species evolved in response to entirely different conditions. The more proper term might be "out of sequence." As a scientific discourse, evolutionary psychology develops a language and set of conceptual categories and methods to puzzle through how humans are out of phase with their historical present moment, how, as an animal on this planet, we have constructed a world that is mismatched or out of tune with our present history. "People have lived," Laland and Brown explain, "in modern societies with agriculture, high population density, and complex social institutions for only a few thousand years, while their predecessors lived in small foraging societies for a much longer period of time. The modern world," they continue, "is very different from that experienced by our genus for most of its two-million-year history."[12] This is an interesting image and gives pause. In a very real sense, today we live in a time out of joint, as it were, as we live modernity's "melting into air" of social conditions with a kind of ineffective skill set hewn out of the glacially creeping process of natural selection. "Psychological mechanisms are assumed to be complex adaptations that evolve slowly and hence that are unlikely to have undergone any significant change since the Pleistocene."[13] That is, modern humans arrive — become "present," as philosophers might say — on the savannah of asphalt and cement with tools for survival from another world. We might say that in a very real sense the tools we have to make our way are already broken, already made to appear odd and "present at hand," as the term goes.

It is in this context we should think of nostalgic return as it applies to *King Lear*. The play registers the past from an analogous early modern evolutionary perspective, bearing witness to how its ennobling values are out of sequence with the play's present. Shakespeare's imagined anachronistic spaces in the play reveal the discord of this patched temporality, its odd dislocations

12 Ibid., 161.
13 Ibid.

seem to litter its narrative landscape. For the reader, the play's placement of modern sentiment within the mythic past of Albion seems to reproduce one of many atonal effects of thematic discord. But to think the play as representing the asequential problem of human evolution appears like the nose on the face of the play's eco-material statements on human existence and survivability. The history of the narrative speaks to this imagined interplay of mismatched chronologies and mixed templates of Stuart economic policy with tribal ritualism, liege relations in a time of Machiavellian rationalism, bourgeois marital spats in the mead hall. Edmund's questions about property and equality seem out of sorts with the play's deeper investment in primogeniture. And the odd nature of familial love ("bias of nature"; 1.2.103) as performance at the beginning of the play — love as a status game about property or love as existential and "real" in a modern inward sense — captures the belated nature of affection within a dynastic family rubbing up against the modern idea of romantic affinity. Also, the sense of friendship in the play seems oddly out of phase: the Fool and Kent are more than servants to the King, but this suggests the idea of duty from another age poorly defines the feelings these characters feel toward Lear. The shifting in proverbial speech, as courtly rhetoric and autonomic reflection, is among these anachronisms. Proverbial language belongs to this earlier phase of evolutionary history, where a world of scarcity and want serves to remind us of our existence on the heath.

What are, finally, the theoretical implications of assigning a recuperative value to mnemonic modes of expression? What does it mean to move to the adage in the context of critical theories of *Lear* and early modern subjectivity? Shakespeare's representation of this mode of expression asks us to rethink the idea of false consciousness as a purely negative critical category. This claim too is not a hugely revelatory idea. In fact, there are classic precedents in critical theory that promote the idea of a "necessary ideology" and "strategic essentialism," or as a starting point to think change. I would argue that in its various forms, this is actually just a clever tailoring of the dialectical charge to place one's critical vocabulary within one's frame of reference as a way to trace how theoretical bias inflects or weighs the objects of concern. Speculative realism might argue that this move to reflect on how our own critical categories shape the way we see the world is just another reenactment of the phenomenological handsaw that posits the object world "outside" one's model is always, to some degree, a projection of the model itself.

Speculative realists might also argue that there is a kind of passive-aggressive element to the self-reflexive critical turn, in that the critical subject — the person doing the theory — only appears to posit their place "within" a model, but in actuality they are preserving both a subject position outside their categories and a privileged space of self-reflection where one "calls the shots," as it were (call it absolute or rational subject, Althusser's scientific Subject), removed from the sphere of influence.[14] A useful analogy can be gleaned from Hollywood digital arts. Speculative realism would argue that phenomenology ends up positing that all approaches to the object world are merely digital images superimposed on the green space. They may have different design programs (theories of the real), but they all end up shaping the image and, finally, seeing what they imagined or constructed in the first place. And this image is finally inclined to reveal when the subject sees itself in its digitally contrived self(imposed)-images. What about the green space itself? The green wall that the images are projected onto? Doesn't it have a reality? A "nature" or set of internally-given patterns that exerts force on the pixels? In response, phenomenologists — or "constructionists" — might argue that this is too simple a characterization of the "science" they apply. They might say, a true scientist has to understand that no matter how you want to render the green space before an image is transposed on it, no matter how you choose to see it (through one's naked eye, a microscope, a

14 See how this argument between dialectical materialism and speculative realism stages each side of the debate in the dialogue between Graham Harman and Slavoj Žižek, as characterized in Harman's account of Žižek's critique in *Tool-Being: Heidegger and the Metaphysics of Objects* (Chicago: Open Court Press, 2002), 206–16.

window, as an algorithm, etc.), all these forms of looking subtly impart a meaning to the object, emphasize one dimension or pattern while downplaying another. Any true "science," as it were, has to take this into account. But the green space as analogy works well to posit the impossibility of ever seeing it, or getting to it, without some method to highlight its own shape or design, since its place in space and time can only be rendered by the pixels that are painted on its non-spatially designed "surface." The new realists would respond, finally, whether we see it or not, it's there, if only in a flash of recognition before it recedes from view.

How this relates to posthuman *Lear* is simple: the posthuman approach favors the speculative turn to realism and focuses on the body as that space where our existence participates with the thing world free of any said conscious manipulation of its process or "being." The body as subject to natural forces outside our control figures in many of the hypothetical examples throughout critics' persistent teasing at the edges of older constructionist perspectives that may privilege the human subject as "anchor" to knowing.[15] As I have been arguing, the Renaissance fascination with memory and proverbs provides an opportunity to reflect on the human as an instance of such enmeshed being where the use of words belongs to something "outside" consciousness, where the habit of articulating memorized patterns of speech works on a somatic level, carvings of past experience on collective codes we inherit as a species. Proverbial speech reveals how our minds work as imprinted machines to recall past prohibitions and useful affective scripts to aid in our in-

---

15 I am building off a considerable scholarship on Shakespeare's idea of the body, especially Gail Kern Paster's observation in *Humoring the Body: Emotions and the Shakespearean Stage* (Chicago: University of Chicago Press, 2004), that the "representation of emotional experience" in his plays, "often in the form of self-report by characters in the throes of strong feeling — presupposed a demonstrable psychophysiological reciprocity between the experiencing subject and his or her relation to the world" (18–19). Paster would say my reading of proverbial voice is a kind of self-report of the Renaissance form of post-traumatic stress.

teraction with the environment. *King Lear's* image of characters retreating to mechanical speech through the proverb overlaps and stands in contrast to some interesting critical readings of the Renaissance interest in automatons.[16] My argument that proverbial speech has a positive value replays many of the earlier dialectical readings to recuperate now fallen or "false" modes of consciousness as potentially necessary or useful.

I want to claim that proverbial speech shows how our bodies work like objects, autonomic reflexes, to relate to our immediate world and gauge the possibility of survival through repetition. To get at the problem of autonomic subjectivity, I will use an example that sits at the heart of modern theories of art. It could be used almost as a test case for my thesis, since it speaks of art's special role in unmasking an unconscious mode of existence. When speaking of the function of art to estrange the real, Viktor Shklovsky in "Art as Technique" uses the rather everyday example from Tolstoy's *Diary*:

> I was cleaning a room and, meandering about, approached the divan and couldn't remember whether or not I had dusted it. Since these movements are habitual and unconscious I could not remember and felt that it was impossible to remember — so that if I had dusted it and forgot — that is, had acted unconsciously, then it was the same as if I had not. If some conscious person had been watching, then the fact could be established. If, however, no one was looking, or looking on unconsciously, if the whole complex lives of many people go on unconsciously, then such lives are as if they had never been.[17]

16 Wendy Beth Hyman, ed., *The Automaton in English Renaissance Literature* (Burlington: Ashgate, 2011). See in particular Brooke Conti, "The Mechanical Saint: Early Modern Devotion and the Language of Automation," 95–108.

17 Victor Shklovsky, "Art as Technique," in *The Critical Tradition: Classic Texts and Contemporary Trends,* ed. David H. Richter (New York: Bedford, 2006), 778.

In this famous passage, Shklovsky takes as his starting point Tolstoy's assessment that one should be alive and self-aware of the domestic chores, without pausing to think that there is a myriad of activities that define modern life that might require a less-than-conscious state in order to suffer through in the first place. There are many minutes in our day where we do exactly what Tolstoy describes: driving a car to work, we reflect on the conversation over breakfast without consciously knowing that we are negotiating traffic, stopping at lights, avoiding injury. Then we realize: how did we get to this intersection? Where did the time go? This example is perhaps indicative of the proverbial "first world problem." And Shklovsky might remind me that it is precisely the routine of a mechanized world that forces such less-than-conscious actions, a world that enslaves us to robotic life.

But we must remember that the characters who are "awake" to the false ideals of their age in Shakespeare's tragedy are the villains. Those who "see" their parts as "loyal son" and "obedient daughter." A good example of this enlivened subjectivity can be found at the end, not in Edmund so much, but in the real agent of Cordelia's death, the assassin Edmund hires. Here we get a good image of someone who has been, in Shklovsky's terms, shocked into an awareness of his moment. Edmund even addresses him as such: "Men / Are as the time is: to be tender-minded / Does not become a sword" (5.3.31–33), Edmund tells him, as if testing to see if he isn't deadened to war already. Privation forces its own form of survival: "I cannot draw a cart, nor eat dried oat. / If it be man's work, I'll do it" (5.3.39–40). The Captain seems to be in full awareness of his senses. One of the darkest thoughts of this tragedy is the definition of the human these lines imply. This character, the Captain, kills to survive. Darker still to imagine that he does this for money. There is humor behind these lines, a humor that defines some of Shakespeare's most cynical thoughts about what it means to be alive during a time of crisis or catastrophe. The Captain cannot eat oats (or is at least damn tired of it), but he can take life. Man's work. Being awake and "enlightened" about one's circumstances does not guarantee a cessation of brutality, or being as hard-stoned as a sword. If there was laughter in the audience at this line when the tragedy was originally performed on the stage, that chortle, I have to think, was intended by Shakespeare and comes from the bleakest realism about human motivation, or what separates domesticated horses and *homo sapiens.*

Shklovsky's theory of *ostranenie,* like Brecht's view of defamiliarization, is predicated upon a liberating form of self-awareness that saves us from the restrictive ideologies of modern bourgeois culture: "And so life is reckoned as nothing. Habitualization devours works, clothes, furniture, one's wife, and the fear of the war."[18] Shklovsky is building off the Aristotelian proviso that "the unexamined life is not worth living." It doesn't occur to Shklovsky that animatronic existence is perhaps the precondition to some forms of labor, that to get through a day's work (making the clothes, the furniture, being conscripted to fight someone else's war) one needs to escape somewhere.[19]

Which is to say that in some instances routine and habituation, or automatic forms of behavior, work as therapeutic tools, coping mechanisms, in response to traumatic experiences. This primal scene of theoretical commonplace could be subject to our own stasis field "transference," if we were to imagine Tolstoy dusting his divan in a bombed-out con-apt in the middle of an urban war zone. This shift in flattening the high aesthetic moment to a kind of real-world ontology should not stretch our imagination. Indeed, such chores and domestic routines do not stop in the middle of brutal skirmishes: parents have to retrieve water and walk to markets while avoiding snipers, children need to be fed, students must attend classes after tsunamis, businesses must open after a virus sweeps through a neighborhood. Living in a world where the everyday is already a visceral shock to one's system — where being "shocked" is already the norm — mod-

18 Ibid.
19 If I am intuiting this correctly, this pushes toward Heideggerian categories — *Zuhandenheit* and *Vorhandenheit* (ready-to-hand, present-to-hand) — to explain a relation to the object world that is perhaps more nuanced than my own.

ernist manifestos might seem like so much background noise, agitprop posters merely redundant, welcome only for their occasion to fuel fire to cook or stay warm.

I said earlier that this cornerstone idea of *ostranenie* (the act of moving someone to self-awareness) might be construed as cruel and unusual punishment if implemented on someone who is really living the circumstances of the heath, where the operation of making the stone stony might be merely a way to remind the dispossessed of the only weapons they have to engage a hostile invading army. Moving one to self-awareness is the unspoken goal of the humanities, seen as a unifying proviso of the liberal arts generally. It is also a keenly revised dogma of humanism's core mission to vitalize the life of the individual student reader: to move to love, work, play and live with a more impassioned sense of purpose and meaning. To live in any other way seems inimical to *being*. This very ideology of humanist practice is predicated on an Anthropocenic bias that may blind us to other values of literary endeavor. As a core mission that goes back at least to the Renaissance humanism, the idea of awakening the reader to their potential through art may itself be "built on sand," as Erasmus might say, at least in the way it appropriates early modern humanism as the headwaters of such idealism. The Renaissance humanists invested deeply in the teaching of language through rote inscription and modeling behavior on emblems, strategies best left unsaid in many modern mission statements clarifying humanist goals. The idea of autonomic behavior targeted by our modern theories of art "as technique" takes for granted that many forms of human behavior are motivated by biological conditions and evolutionary adaptations to begin with.[20]

---

20 If we want a proverbial image, think of Polonius in *Hamlet* giving his son Laertes the "precepts" to memorize and follow so that after he departs he can live caringly and earnestly: "Neither a lender nor a borrower be" (1.3.75). Polonius thinks he may never see his son again (which turns out to be the case). Remember these. Character them. Polonius may be a dim wit, a kind of a laughable humanist, really. But it is hard to argue that his advice is bad.

Consider that this form of autonomic action is precisely at the center of defining the human for Karl Popper in his *Knowledge and the Body–Mind Problem* in his own parable of the centipede in the epigraph above. For Popper, the routine of physical work is a "low order" form of human behavior, and like the animal whose body is "parallel" to its mind and works in conjunction to effect its existence. When the centipede is asked to think about walking, the very act of mobility is frozen by his self-awareness. Like many parables, this story is absurd because it features an insect acting human and engaging in "shop talk" with another multiply-limbed arthropod. But it sets up an interesting paradox that allows us to return to the very question of animatronic action as a way to save the category of the human. Adolph Busch's exceedingly rich artistic practice is meant to embody the nobility of human achievement, yet its very possibility relies on unself-conscious rote habit. Busch, it appears, can only be a supreme example of human art and music when being centipede-like, when being animal. When asked to think like a spider— or to be self-aware ("human")— his violin concerto ceases, never to be heard again, except perhaps as its own adage here for us about the importance of becoming human (or centipede) through inhuman unconscious action.

Perhaps the way to see Popper's parable is to imagine that we become human paradoxically through returning to an earlier posthuman state. Busch's story troubles the very high-low categories Popper tries to assert in his reflection on parallelism.

Even if Spinoza is right, and even if electrons have their subjective states, it is not really what we are after. This kind of momentary consciousness is so far removed from what we are interested in that the problem of evolution certainly still exists. That is to say, the problem then is how do we get from the electron state of consciousness to the human state of consciousness? And that can be explained by evolution. So even if we accept Spinoza's similar parallelistic theory, all the problems remain. They are not really in any way solved. We will never know about the insight of electrons— actu-

ally, even the electrons do not know ... If there is parallelism — if mind and body do run parallel — then connected
consciousness would be a kind of memory, and this can be
parallel only to a physical system that has memory. Now
many physical systems have memory. For example, magnets have memory. So physical systems pretty far removed
from life have memory. Probably all crystals have memory,
and magnets have memory ... Animals have it already, and
have had it for ever so many millions of years. So it is likely
genetically based.[21]

Before wincing at the idea of material rocks having memory — druidic crystals with animistic powers — think of simple
examples where a species' instincts are "written" in the carbon
chains of the newly born animal's DNA. How does the experiential memory of one animal get transferred to its young? Fledg-
ling ducks hatch with the behavior to follow (or model) the first
image of adult-duck being they trip upon. Ready to wean on
eucalyptus, baby koalas crawl out of their mother's pouch with
the instinct to eat koala feces so that their stomachs can acquire
the bacteria needed to then digest the otherwise poisonous
leaves. (Koalas are one of the only animals on earth to live on
one food source.) These two examples demonstrate forms of behavior that, on the surface, might seem to jeopardize the safety
of the newly born creature, but in fact they become an adaptive
behavior upon which the species thrives. Countless examples
of animal behavior come to mind that lend credence to a parallelism between the behavior and its rocky inscription in the
crystal-like gene code.

The proverb is that linguistic inscription that defines the
equivalent of such imprinting; the action of the past is set for
modeling in the mnemonic recall. Proverbial speech marks the
fine line where the human lives in this evolutionary "space" between the thing world and its reflective subjectivity, between the
two "higher" and "lower" orders existing in a parallel state, to use

21   Popper, *Knowledge and the Body-Mind Problem*, 121–22.

Popper's hierarchy. Human reflection on past actions is etched upon the stone of collective memory that lives on through the generations to later activate autonomic cues, where the subject talks to itself in its own/other voice: instructions for survival, wisdom, perseverance, for patience against the storm, for calm, or to have a good laugh at the odds. Unlike Popper, though, I am not saying that "adage-ntial" subjectivity is another indicator of our placement above or over the rocks and animals of the world, but rather marks the realm where language of the past antici-pates human action in the present.

Take a real-world example that brings us back to proverbs and the idea of survival. In a compelling study of women in war-torn Palestine, Nadera Shalhoub-Kevorkian focuses on the cop-ing strategies of mothers and wives dealing with keeping their families together while loved ones are imprisoned or killed. How did they deal with the trauma? Shalhoub-Kevorkian writes:

> Sharing worries with the group helped the women to cope with their difficult emotions. For example, when some of the women expressed feelings of guilt for not being able to stop the trauma, others immediately responded with such comments as "There is a limit to our power or ability to help," "We never stopped searching for ways of preventing such trauma," and, "My screaming was the only weapon to fight them back, and I used it." I remember hearing an Arabic proverb repeatedly: "Ma bi'einak ala il murr illa il ammar minnuh" (Nothing can help you cope with bitter pain, except your knowledge that it can be worse). Thus cultural norms, beliefs, and even the comfort of proverbs were used as tools to reduce pain, diminish suffering, and help in coping with anxiety, depression, hopelessness, and helplessness.[22]

---

22 Shalhoub-Kevorkian, "Voice Therapy for Women Aligned with Political Prisoners: A Case Study of Trauma among Palestinian Women in the Sec-ond Intifada," *Social Service Review* 79.2 (2005): 322–43.

Erasmus would find Shalhoub-Kevorkian's observations affirming. He would be keenly interested in the Arabic proverb, as he would say it bears a striking resemblance to Seneca. "That life has its evils, and that they more than balance its comforts, is pretty generally admitted; yet we find that even a long continuance of pain and distress have not the power, in many of us, of weaning us from it. Seneca makes one of his characters say, 'Take from me the use of my hands and of my feet, dash out my teeth, and inflict upon me a thousand other ills, preserve but my life, and I will still be contented.'"[23] Drawing upon this frame offered by Shalhoub-Kevorkian, we can return to the image of citational speech as more of a survival strategy. Importantly, her patients "remember hearing" the proverb, but not saying it. Speaking out of reflex as a form of existing on the heath, now means to seek solace and collective wisdom in the face of potential demise: listening to oneself speak in the position of the other.

King Lear's narrative strategy is to ask the audience to cringe at the misplaced retribution leveled at main characters. But I believe it also calls for us to see the restorative effects of ingrained behavioral mechanisms. In response to Cordelia's death, and seeking comfort in the somnambulant rhythms of citational adage, Albany cries: "All friends shall taste / The wages of their virtue, and all foes / The cup of their deserving" (5.3.301–3). The proverbial effect of the lines — "wages of virtue" and "cup of deserving" — seem to perfectly misread how the plot plays out for all of its surviving characters. The lines seem so utterly off the mark: how can Shakespeare possibly think that the waste on the stage signals anything close to evidence of supernatural justice? Doesn't the scene demand a sympathetic read? I would argue that these lines, as suggested in our example of the wives and daughters of political prisoners of the intifada, reveal how characters seek emotional closure through the process of commemorating their experiences. Albany is allowed through the citational quality of the speech to remove himself from the pre-

---

23 Desiderius Erasmus, *Proverbs Chiefly Taken from the Adagia of Erasmus,* ed. Robert Bland (London: T. Egerton, 1814), 284–85.

sent and seek possible refuge. To rush to the scene and shake Albany, to wake him up, to tell him he's merely dusting a divan without thought, lost in ideology, falsely conscious in routine, is to be as harsh as the stones that litter the beach at his feet.

In response, Lear asks his final question about the value of human life. It is posited like one of the relational lists known to thing theorists for the way it conjures an assemblage of agents by implying a network of causality. Yet in this instance, the list recounts the limit boundary or flat horizon of mortality that levels not just all social distinctions, but all animate objects: "Why should a dog, a horse, a rat, have life / And thou no breath at all?" (5.3.305–6). When he dies, Kent responds, "Vex not his ghost. O let him pass! He hates him much / That would upon the rack of this tough world / Stretch him out longer" (5.3.312–14). The lines could be read in our context against the strain of modernist appeals to stir the subject from its existence.

This is the End: Repurposing Fatalism

> By the constant trickling of water, the solid stone becomes excavated.
> — Erasmus, *Adages*[24]

I started this book with an epigraph from Rilke, a passage I came upon myself while reading Amitav Ghosh's marvelous novel, *The Hungry Tide*. It is in a scene from a notebook scrawled by an older character, Nirmal Bose, who has given up his dream of being a poet to work in the countryside as a teacher, in the Sundarban effluvial islands of the Ganges in the Bay of Bengal. In a remarkable scene, he has been told that a band of peasants who have settled the islands to farm and fish will most likely be evicted and possibly killed by the government because the land has been declared an ecological preserve. Nirmal sees in this settlement an image of his earlier socialist politics, the chance to forge a new society based on egalitarianism and promise. He

24 Ibid., 65.

meets an old colleague at a festival meant to introduce the new village to dignitaries and intellectuals from Calcutta. Nirmal's notebook recounts the scene:

> "I know a couple of them," I said. "Now that I'm almost retired, I'm thinking of doing some teaching here."
>
> "Here?" he said dubiously. "But the problem is, they may not be allowed to stay."
>
> "They're here already," I said. "How could they be evicted now? There would be bloodshed."
>
> He laughed. "My friend, have you forgotten what we used to say in the old days?"
>
> "What?"
>
> "You cannot make an omelet without breaking eggs."
>
> He laughed in the cynical way of those who, having never believed in the ideals they once professed, imagine that no one else had done so either. I was tempted to tell him what I thought of him, but it struck me with great force that I had no business to be self-righteous about these matters. Nilima — she had achieved a great deal. What had I done? What was the work of my life? I tried to find an answer but none would come to mind.[25]

Right after this scene, Nirmal sees a fisherman catching crabs in the bay: "As I watch him," Nirmal reflects,

> my heart spills over, There is so much to say, so much in my head, so much that will remain unsaid. Oh those wasted years, that wasted time. I think of Rilke going for years without writing a word and then, in a matter of weeks, producing the *Duino Elegies*.[26]

It's a compelling scene, where the sight of a fisherman playing with his nets provides a formative image for man who believes

25 Amitav Ghosh, *The Hungry Tide* (New York: Houghon Mifflin, 2005), 160.
26 Ibid. Emphasis original.

his own life has been wasted in dreaming, but also feeling re-vitalized with an image of a revolution that he can believe in. Images of productive labor to a poet who feels, given his po-litical and aesthetic convictions, that he has lost his youth: the two catalysts for the epiphany are that his older revolutionary colleague admits he never believed in his ideals to begin with (hence making it easy for him to side with the government who will now crush the settlement of workers) and this image of the fisherman engaged in the simplicity of work. The chapter ends:

> How better can we praise the world but by doing what the Poet would have us do: by speaking of potters and rope makers, by telling of

> *Some simple thing shaped for generation after generation until it lives in our hands and in our eyes, and it's ours.*[27]

Nirmal is heartened by the image of simple craft, a base art of sorts, that fuses for him his sense of community and mission as a poet. Nirmal could be a loose symbol for the Western intellec-tual looking to seek his or her way in the "divide" between meas-uring one's older communal social politics with the idealism offered in this image of returning to the "simple thing shaped for generation after generation." Ghosh's *Hungry Tide* applies directly to the challenge of the new materialism's rethinking of our older ideals and social commitments as progressive human-ists. Its plot hinges on the problem of weighing the safety of the rural poor with that of saving endangered animals and their environment. This is graphically illustrated in the novel's depic-tion of the Morichijhanpi massacre (1978–79), where the West Bengal government brutally evicted and ultimately starved to death the Bengali refugees in a socialist-run settler camp on a nature preserve. This story is told in conjunction with the story of a young marine biologist whose discovery in the area of the river dolphin, *Orcaella brevirostris,* asks the reader to weigh the

27 Ibid. Emphasis original.

idealism of a Western ecologist's concerns for the environment with the real-life needs of the people who live in the Sundarbans. The novel's investment in thinking through both sides of the argument could be described as a classic example of the early modern humanist's practice of *intramque partem* (this side and the other), where students were asked to write out dialogues from both perspectives on controversial topics.[28] In one pivotal scene from novel, Piya, the young marine biologist, witnesses a village kill a tiger who has trapped itself in a stable. Tigers are portrayed throughout the novel as menacing and destructive: a darker force of nature that is responsible for thousands of deaths in the area every year. But for Piya, the tiger is a beautiful animal and should be preserved. The tiger's slaughter is unsettling to her, and she later argues with a friend from the area, Kanai, who, like her, is educated and an outsider to the rural community. Piya is haunted by the "horror" of the villagers' behavior:

> "Last night: I still can't get it out of my head… That's what haunts me," said Piya. "In a way that makes them part of the horror too, doesn't it?"…
>
> "That tiger had killed two people, Piya," Kanai said. "And that was just in one village. It happens every week that people are killed by tigers. How about the horror of that? If there were killing on that scale anywhere else on earth it would be called a genocide, and yet here it goes almost unremarked: these killings are never reported, never written about in papers. And the reason is just that these people are too poor to matter. We all know it, but we choose not to see it. Isn't that a horror too — that we can feel the suffering of an animal, but not of human beings?"

---

28 See Joel Altman's *The Tudor Play of Mind: Rhetorical Inquiry and the Development of Elizabethan Drama* (Berkeley: University of California Press, 1978) for an exploration of this rhetorical exercise as a foundation to Renaissance poetic aesthetics.

"But Kanai," Piya retorted, "everywhere in the world dozens of people are killed every day — on roads, in cars, in traffic. Why is this any worse?"

"Because we're complicit in this, Piya, that's why."

Piya dissociated herself with a shake of the head. "I don't see how I'm complicit."

"Because it was people like you," said Kanai, "who made a push to protect the wildlife here, without regard for the human costs. And I'm complicit because people like me — Indians of my class, that is — have chosen to hide these costs, basically in order to curry favor with their Western patrons. It's not hard to ignore the people who're dying — after all, they are the poorest of the poor. But just ask yourself if this would be allowed to happen anywhere else. There are more tigers living in America, in captivity, then there are in all of India — what do you think would happen if they started killing human beings?"

"The difference, Kanai," Piya said slowly and emphatically, "is that it was what was intended — not by you or me, but by nature, by the earth, by the planet that keeps us all alive. Just suppose we crossed that imaginary line that prevents us from deciding that no other species matters except ourselves. What'll be left then? Aren't we alone enough in the universe? And do you think it'll stop at that? Once we decide we can kill off other species, it'll be people next — just the kind of people you're thinking of, people who're poor and unnoticed."[29]

For those invested in the ecological turns in literary criticism, this is an arresting scene because it depicts so honestly the discursive limits of the thorny ethical divide that separates two forms of progressive political concerns currently animating cultural studies in the humanities. This scene, like the image of the tiger's demise, lingers in the reader's memory and does not too easily disappear in the novel's careful resolutions.

29 Ghosh, *The Hungry Tide*, 248–49.

Isn't this the dilemma of eco-materialism's appropriation of literary texts as a vehicle to speak to the potential, but also the futility, of imagining "our" sustainable future? I want to say a bit more about the challenge of this theory to offer a present eco-politics. It is hard not to read some of the new material-ism as fatalist in its assertion of human agency in the face of the global scale of present ecological problems. While I iden-tify with the eco-materialism, I do believe it is difficult to deter-mine the cultural politics of its push against the old materialist emphasis on social differences based on binaries of power re-lations, human rights, moral debts, alienation of laborers, and the suffering of the poor. The fact that this list feels "old" or "so twentieth-century" in its telling is perhaps more a problem of the commodity logic of literary criticism, where one is pushed to repackage, find new shelf space, for one's work by rebranding it (or another instance of professional indifference: "we already did 'suffering of the poor,' I want readings that tell me something new"). Needless to say, eco-materialism can appear to some as overtly misanthropic in its lack of concern for those humans in the developing world who are faced with wanting to survive by adapting to first world farming technologies (using nitrogen-based fertilizer to enhance production of arable land, say, but in doing so then facing the consequences of polluting runoff water with resulting algal blooms). Only the most hard-hearted of first world academics would care more for the algae as "thing" than the parent faced with feeding their child or polluting the sea.

Another way to make visible the riddle of reading the poli-tics of eco-materialism is to imagine a right-wing think tank using the argument of flat ontology to challenge the argument of global warming. The denial of human agency can mean one thing in the context of challenging the Kantian propositions of revisionist historicism, quite another if made in front of a Sen-ate Committee in charge of determining who is responsible for the oil spill or lead in the city water. We might identify this con-tradiction as the effect of emphasis in new materialism's push-ing back on the "subjectivist potency" of rational awareness (a kind of fractal "magic bullet" theory of global catastrophe — but now "magic butterfly" — that is, "a butterfly somewhere on the other side of the planet flapped its wings, and that is why we did not apply quality control, Senator"). If the new materialism's seemingly over-emphasis on downplaying human agency (the so-called "democratization of things" applied to causality at the quantum level) is read by some as a diversionary tactic that means to distract us from thinking about the role we actually do play in the Anthropocene, then it is because there is a rigorous tendency to rewrite the critical-theoretical trespasses of the past by clinging steadfastly to the idea of the "imminent" multiply-determined causes beyond the influence of mere simple modes of redress or adaptability. Though we might admire the tenacity of those who work hard to assert the complexity of our "enmeshed" existence, I do feel nonetheless that some proverbial cautions about theoretical overreach may apply to our own rethinking.[30] Jameson's response to Foucault's *Discipline and Punish* as displaying a "winner loses logic," for example, can be directed at some of new materialism's emphasis, what he called the "strange quasi-Sartrean irony — a 'winner loses logic' — which tends to surround any effort to describe a 'system;'

30 Rosi Braidotti's chapter "Post-Humanism: Life Beyond the Self" in *The Posthuman* (Cambridge: Polity Press, 2013) provides one of the best historical summaries of posthuman discourses growing out of critiques of political blind spots in European leftist theory since World War II. See also her honest critical appraisal of object-oriented philosophy in "Borrowed Energy: Interview," in *Frieze* 165 (Sept. 2014): http://www.frieze.com/issue/article/borrowed-energy/. She says, "There are two or three things that I don't fully get about the speculative realists. First of all, the treatment of objects as self-organizing entities is not in itself new. Media and science fiction scholars — like Jussi Parikka now, or Donna Haraway before him — have been theorizing objects along these lines for years. Similarly, the emphasis on matter, and the continuity between matter and mind, and between human bodies and the world in which they live, is not new either. It has always been at the core of Spinozist, Deleuzian and materialist feminist studies, including those of Simone de Beauvoir, Haraway and my own. I am surprised, sometimes even shocked, that their discussions and bibliographies make little mention of these debates. How can you wipe out the whole of Deleuzian studies in one footnote? 'The Deleuzian quest, even process ontology really, is correlationist.' Excuse me? What are you saying? ... I can only describe this in terms of a political economy of negative affects."

a totalizing dynamic, as these are detected in the movement of contemporary society." His own advice can be seen as proverbial to the new generation:

> What happens is that the more powerful the vision of some increasingly total system or logic — the Foucault of the prisons book is the obvious example — the more powerless the reader comes to feel. Insofar as the theorist wins, therefore, by constructing an increasingly closed and terrifying machine, to that very degree he loses, since the critical capacity of his work is thereby paralyzed, and the impulses of negation and revolt, not to speak of those of social transformation, are increasingly perceived as vain and trivial in the face of the model itself.[31]

Jameson asks: who wins if we paint through our theory and critical categories of inquiry an enmeshed existence that seems bound, Sisyphus-like, to changing what we have already portrayed as an inalterable set of conditions?

And, let's face it; it is easy to paint these conditions. Consider just one industry and its carbon output: according to one estimate, there are 93,000 airline flights around the world every day. An airplane like Rolls Royce's A380 uses as much fuel as 3,500 family cars.

> A single round trip flight from New York to Europe or San Francisco produces two to three tons of carbon dioxide per person. To put this in perspective, the average American generates 19 tons of carbon dioxide and the average European produces ten *over the entire year*. A few flights, in other words, can completely overwhelm any attempts to reduce your personal contribution to global warming.[32]

31 Fredric Jameson, *Postmodernism, or, The Cultural Logic of Late Capitalism* (Durham: Duke University Press, 1991), http://xroads.virginia.edu/~drbr/ jameson/jameson.html.

32 "Issue Briefing: Impacts of Airplane Pollution on Climate Change and Health," in *Flying Clean: Campaign to Cut Air Pollution,* http://www.flying-

Or, to put this succinctly, without shutting down air travel, the individual efforts we all make to reduce carbon, sadly, do not really matter. There is very little that can be done to alter the jet engine to effect the amount of fuel needed to maintain air transport, nor is there going to be, in the near future, a curtailing of air travel in the proceeding decades of global capitalist expansion. If anything, the industry will grow 5% per year, doubling by one estimation its output in fifteen years, and tripling it in twenty-three.[33]

One of the rhetorical effects of eco-materialism is to invoke apocalypse as a means to proffer the value of its otherwise measured claims about the value of its endeavors. In research, books, conferences, apocalypse sells. It is to ecological studies what pornography is to some feminist criticism: a way to both claim an ethical target while ensuring an audience through amplifying the political stakes. (Another way to put this might be to say, you don't really need to argue anything when talking about apocalypse or porn, since you already have the audience's attention... just show clips).

It is a rhetorical technique I admittedly claim to be doing right now (and throughout this book). But this shouldn't be seen as planting red herrings in our seed rows, or avoiding the deeper core values of our critical labor. I can think of no other context we should rather be thinking about when reading and teaching literature and philosophy. Apocalypse sells itself. But on this score, much of the academic frenzy that is "apocalypse now" seems to replay another Renaissance trope of adopting melancholic affect, which, if true, can only contain such new and otherwise inspired readings of our cherished texts as forms of narcissistic performative gestures. I hope my own work avoids this trap. Piya's argument, I must admit, does not too easily wither in the face of the argument that modernization and

clean.com/impacts_airplane_pollution_climate_change_and_health. Emphasis mine. See also "Aircraft Emissions: The Sky's the Limit," *The Economist,* June 8, 2006.

33 "Issue Briefing."

progress should trump ecology when thinking of the rights of individuals living in the developing world. We have to remember that the adage about breaking eggs to make an omelet in Ghosh's story comes from someone in a position of state power to assert the conservation of the Sundarban archipelago. This is prodigal rhetoric like that of Goneril and Regan, using proverbial speech to advance a dubious political claim and hide one's real professional commitments — getting published, advancing our careers — under the guise of eco-politics. Ghosh wants us to side with Piya, I feel, but also to see the heartless treatment of the settlers for what it is, a power grab meant to put down a people whose socialist politics reveal the weakness and broken ideals of those in power.

What will be the role of literature in this new world, which seems on the face of it for many to belong to the prodigal world of leisure and excess? Ghosh's novel seems to be a direct response to this question: his narrative solution is an imagined one, its own ideological resolution, but it is carefully moving toward a synthesis of the two entangled arguments of eco- and social-progressive alternatives. Repurposing fatalism means finding the middle ground between the two positions, reclaiming the utopian dialectics of the former while keeping our eye on the scientific realities of raising our children, nieces and nephews, and grandchildren with diminishing resources. To do this we'll need to repurpose our fatalism by adapting to the new environments and changing conditions presented to us in the twenty-first century. At the end, the reader is thrilled as consumer of fiction but also informed historically about the people and mangrove forests of the Ganges delta. To put a book down and read the world differently through an ecological lens seems a decent starting point.

I think there is a place for returning to Kenneth Burke's formulation of literary narrative operating as proverbial caution and ethical mapping. Ethical mapping is my term, but it works nicely with Ian Hodder's idea in his *Entangled: An Archeology of the Relationships between Humans and Things,* to think how literacy as a social practice is "entangled" within ecologically diminished zones and habitats. For Hodder, the dominant narrative about human adaptation and evolution is about our ability to work within a quite narrow range of environmental limits, particular "niches" with their own set of demands. He calls this set of behavioral adaptation "fittingness," where a particular attribute that has been etched into our behavioral skill set comes to "'fit' or 'come into play' in specific historical contexts."[34] Hodder wants this idea to maintain the two senses of the term "to adapt to an end or design" and to "harmonize with." One of the key practices Hodder examines is that of mimesis, to "make, use and reproduce things using routine practices … at the same time dealing with broader goals and purposes." He writes: "Highly active and situational mimetic and transformative processes work within corpuses of objects that have their traditions and ways of doing things."[35] The emphasis here is on human traditions offering what Hodder sees as a "coherence" with labor or vocation across temporal locations. Hegel might see this as a bare art: "humans get caught up," Hodder explains, "in the attempt to make links across domains, to create intellectual coherence, to seek metaphor and unity of idea."[36] Another key term for Hodder is that of "synaesthesia," quoting the work of Brent Berlin and E.H. Gombrich to define the "The representation of … lip and tongue movements in [our] motor brain maps may be mapped in non-arbitrary ways to certain sound inflections in auditory regions [of the brain] and the latter, in turn, function as non-arbitrary links to an object's visual appearance."[37] Usually regarded, Hodder notes, quoting Christopher Tilley, "as a peculiar, romantic or even pathological experience," the idea of synaesthesia being the root-node of human behavior can "instead be regarded as our primordial preconceptual experience

34 Ian Hodder, *Entangled: An Archeology of the Relationships between Humans and Things* (Malden: Wiley Blackwell, 2012), 113–14.
35 Ibid., 123.
36 Ibid.
37 Ibid., 125.

of the world."[38] Hodder's idea of a human's seeking ways to think of relatedness to objects through the simple routine of repeating sounds to trigger "links" and thereby make intelligible our environment sounds familiar enough to a Renaissance humanist approach to "character" (memorize) maxims for later use. Hodder's *Entangled* offers a utopian image of possibility through human adaption.

We can return to Gaia Vince's *Adventures in the Anthropocene* for another image of our intrepid species. Vince refuses to give into the pessimism of her own grim accounting of the first world's consumption of natural resources and the daily struggle of those who live in poor communities. Many of her examples are of local heroism where courage and innovation win the day — finding ways for villages to keep glaciers from thawing in Nepal, or inventing new crops to keep consistent yields in Uganda, finding ways to live on rivers that really do flow upstream (literally), whose dams produce needed electricity but take away fishing — where new technologies and means of adapting and countering effects of crisis come to read like a book of exemplars. Her optimism is not forced, it is based on the facts of the case:

> And yet, for all our observations, for all our technological advances and modeling expertise, the future has never been harder to predict. Our threats are many, including much of what we are bringing on ourselves — but we are resourceful, intelligent and endlessly adaptable. As we enter the Anthropocene, our species has never had it so good — more of us than ever are living longer and better. We have the medical and technological knowledge, and logistical ability to improve the lives of poor, hungry and sick people everywhere. And that power doesn't stop with our human world, of course; we could have a similarly positive effect on our wild world ... the extraordinary diversity of life created through

---

38 Ibid., quoting Christopher Tilley, *The Materiality of Stone: Explorations in Landscape Phenomenology* (Oxford: Berg Publishers, 2004).

millions of years of physical, chemical and evolutionary processes ... Now that we are aware of our impacts, we are the first species to be in a position to choose the future of our planet. I fervently hope we choose a shared future.[39]

To live, to survive, we will need to invent new categories of thought to value what has been, until now, unseen shapes and forms of existence(s). Adapting is one of the things we do as a species. We are good at it. In Hodder's terms, our ability to adapt hinges on our reliance on entangled being coded in "primordial preconceptual experience." Our ability to relate to our object world through proverbial cues defines this inhuman reflex: to call to mind any number of affective responses urging us how to live in accord with the world, to recall and interface with the toolbox of being passed to us in our collective history — moments of labor, craft, biological or economic reproduction, travel. We will change. Adapt. But wisely. "Well begun is half done." "Make haste slowly," Erasmus might say. We will not be alone on the heath.

39 Gaia Vince, *Adventures in the Anthropocene: A Journey to the Heart of the Planet We Made* (London: Chatto and Windus, 2014), 380–81.

BIBLIOGRAPHY

Agamben, Giorgio. *The Open: Man and Animal*. Trans. Kevin Attell. Stanford: Stanford University Press, 2004.

"Aircraft Emissions: The Sky's the Limit." *The Economist*, June 8, 2006. http://www.economist.com/node/7033931.

Albala, Ken. *The Banquet: Dining in the Great Courts of Late Renaissance Europe*. Chicago: University of Illinois Press, 2007.

Altman, Joel. *The Tudor Play of Mind: Rhetorical Inquiry and the Development of Elizabethan Drama*. Berkeley and Los Angeles: University of California Press, 1978.

"Ancient Stone Markers Warned of Tsunamis." *CBS News*, April 6, 2011. http://www.cbsnews.com/news/ancient-stone-markers-warned-of-tsunamis/.

Appleby, Stuart. *Famine in Tudor and Stuart England*. Stanford: Stanford University Press, 1978.

Arnold, Matthew. "Dover Beach." 1867. In *Selected Poems*, ed. Timothy Peltason. New York: Penguin Classic, 1995.

Aska. "Aneyoshi tsunami warning stone tablet." *Megalithic Portal*, June 22, 2013. http://www.megalithic.co.uk/article.php?sid=34248.

Ast, Dieter G., Michael Brill, Ward Goodenough, Maureen Kaplan, Frederick Newmeyer, Woodruff Sullivan, Victor R. Baker, et al. "Excerpts from *Expert Judgment on Markers to Deter Inadvertent Human Intrusion into the Waste Isolation Pilot Plant*" [*sic*]. http://downlode.org/Etext/WIPP/.

Aubrey, John. *Brief Lives*. Ed. Richard Barber. Woodbridge: Boydell, 1982.

Beier, A.L. *Masterless Men: The Vagrancy Problem in England*. London: Methuen, 1985.

Bell, Millicent. *Shakespeare's Tragic Skepticism*. New Haven: Yale University Press, 2002.

Benjamin, Walter. *Illuminations*. Trans. Harry Zohn. New York: Schocken Books, 1969.

Bennett, Jane. *Vital Matter: A Political Ecology of Things*. Durham, NC: Duke University Press, 2010.

Berland, Kevin. "Bribing Aristophanes: The Uses of History and the Attack on the Theater in England." In *Sustaining Literature: Essays on Literature, History, and Culture, 1500-1800*, ed. Greg Clingham, 229–46. Lewisburg, PA: Bucknell University Press, 2007.

Boeher, Bruce. *Shakespeare Among the Animals: Nature and Society in the Drama of Early Modern England*. Basingstoke: Palgrave Macmillan, 2002.

Bogost, Ian. *Alien Phenomenology: or What It's Like To Be A Thing*. Minneapolis: Minnesota University Press, 2012.

Bradley, A.C. *Shakespearean Tragedy: Lectures on Hamlet, Othello, King Lear, Macbeth*. London: Macmillan, 1905.

Bradshaw, Graham. *Shakespeare's Scepticism*. New York: St. Martin Press, 1987.

Braidotti, Rosi. "Borrowed Energy: Interview." *Frieze* 165 (Sept. 2014).

———. *The Posthuman*. Cambridge: Polity Press, 2013.

Bristol, Michael. "Theater and Popular Culture." In *A New History of Early English Drama*, ed. John D. Cox and David Scott Kastan, 231–51. New York: Columbia University Press, 1997.

Buesseler, Ken O., Steven R. Jayne, Nicholas S. Fisher, Irina I. Rypina, Hannes Baumann, Zofia Baumann, Crystaline F. Breier, et al. "Fukushima-derived Radionuclides in the Ocean and Biota off Japan." *Proceedings of the National Academy of Sciences* 109.16 (2012): 5984-88. DOI: 10.1073/pnas.1120794109. http://www.pnas.org/content/109/16/5984.

Burke, Kenneth. *The Philosophy of Literary Form: Studies in Symbolic Action*. New York: Vintage Books, 1941.

Burke, Peter. *The Historical Anthropology of Early Modern Italy: Essays on Perception and Communication*. Cambridge: Cambridge University Press, 2005.

Bushnell, Rebecca. *A Culture of Teaching: Early Modern Humanism in Theory and Practice*. Ithaca: Cornell University Press, 1996.

Carroll, Joseph. "An Evolutionary Approach to Shakespeare's *King Lear*." In *Critical Insights: Family*, ed. John Knapp. Ipswich, MA: *EBSCO*, 2012.

Carroll, William C. *Fat King, Lean Beggar: Representations of Poverty in the Age of Shakespeare*. Ithaca: Cornell University Press, 1996.

Cavell, Stanley. "The Avoidance of Love: A Reading of *King Lear*." In *Disowning Knowledge in Seven Plays of Shakespeare*. Cambridge: Cambridge University Press, 2003.

Chew, Audrey. *Stoicism in Renaissance English Literature*. New York: Peter Lang, 1988.

Claesz, Pieter. *Still Life*. 1625/30. Art Institute of Chicago. *Art Institute of Chicago*. http://www.artic.edu/aic/collections/artwork/21682.

———. *Still Life with a Turkey Pie*. 1627. Rijksmuseum, Amsterdam. *Wikimedia Commons*. https://commons.wikimedia.org/wiki/File: Still_Life_with_Turkey_Pie_1627_Pieter_Claesz.jpg.

Cohen, Jeffrey. *Stone: An Ecology of the Inhuman*. Minneapolis: University of Minnesota, 2015.

———. "Time out of Memory." In *Posthistorical Middle Ages*, eds. Elizabeth Scala and Sylvia Federico. London: Palgrave, 2009.

Coole, Diana and Samantha Frost, ed. *New Materialisms: Ontology, Agency, and Politics*. Durham: Duke University Press, 2010.

Cosmides, L. and J. Tooby. "From Evolution to Behavior: Evolutionary Psychology as the Missing Link." In *The Latest and The Best Essays on Evolution and Optimality*, ed. J. Dupre, 280–81. Cambridge: MIT Press, 1987.

Cox, John. *Seeming Knowledge: Shakespeare and Skeptical Faith*. Waco, TX: Baylor University Press, 2007.

Crutzen, P.J. "Geology of Mankind." *Nature* 415.6867 (2002): 23.

Curry, Andrew. "Gobekli Tepe: The World's First Temple?" *Smithsonian Magazine*, Nov. 2008. http://www.smithsonianmag.com/history/gobekli-tepe-the-worlds-first-temple-83613665/.

DeLanda, Manuel. *Intensive Science and Virtual Philosophy*. New York: Continuum Press, 2005.

Deleuze, Gilles. *Difference and Repetition*. Trans. Paul Patton. London: Athlone Press, 1997.

Dent, Alan. *World of Shakespeare: Animals & Monsters*. New York: Taplinger, 1972.

Dent, R.W. *Shakespeare's Proverbial Language: An Index*. Berkeley: University of California Press, 1981.

Dionne, Craig. "'Now For the Lords' Sake': Vagrancy, Downward Mobility, and Low Aesthetics." Special issue on "Vagrant Subjects," *Early Modern Culture Electronic Seminar* 7 (2008). http://emc.eserver.org/1-7/dionne_response.html.

———— and Steve Mentz, ed. *Rogues and Early Modern Literary Culture*. Ann Arbor: University of Michigan Press, 2004.

Dollimore, Jonathan. *Radical Tragedy: Religion, Ideology and Power in the Drama of Shakespeare and his Contemporaries*. Chicago: University of Chicago Press, 1984.

Duncan-Jones, Katherine. *Shakespeare: Upstart Crow to Sweet Swan, 1592-1623*. London: Methuen Drama, 2011.

Eagleton, Terry. *Sweet Violence: The Idea of the Tragic*. London: Wiley-Blackwell, 2002.

Edelman, Charles. "Shakespeare and the Invention of the Epic Theater: Working with Brecht." *Shakespeare Survey* 58 (2005): 130–36.

Eden, Kathy. *Friends Hold All Things in Common: Tradition, Intellectual Property, and the Adages of Erasmus*. New Haven: Yale University Press, 2001.

Elton, William. King Lear *and the Gods*. Chicago: Huntington Library, 1966.

Elyot, Thomas. *Bankette of Sapience. Compyled By Syr Thomas Elyot Knyght, and Newly Augmented With Dyuerse Titles [et] Sentences*. Londini: In ædibus Thomæ Bertheleti typis impress. Cum priuilegio ad imprimendum solum, 1542.

Erasmus (Desiderius Erasmus Roterodamus). *The Adages of Erasmus*. Ed. William Barker. Toronto: Toronto University Press, 2001.

———. *Adagiorum*. 1518. Trans. and annot. R. A. B. Mynors. Toronto & Buffalo: University of Toronto Press, 1991.

———. "*Paupertas sapientiam sportia est.*" *Collected Works of Erasmus: Adages: II1 to IV100*. Ed. Margaret Phillips and R.A.B. Mynors. Toronto: University of Toronto Press, 1982.

———. *Proverbs Chiefly Taken from the Adagia of Erasmus*. Vol. I. Ed. Robert Bland. London: T. Egerton, 1814.

Fackler, Martin. "Tsunami Warnings Written in Stone." *The New York Times*, April 20, 2012. https://heka.files.wordpress.com/2012/03/on-stones-in-japan-tsunami-warnings-e28094-aneyoshi-journal-nytimes-20110420.pdf.

Fauvre, Ashle. "Tsunami." Soaking in Japan (blog), May 14, 2011. http://soakinginjapan.blogspot.jp/2011/05/tsunami.html.

Foster, Marc, dir. *World War Z*. Paramount Pictures, 2013.

Freeman, Lisa. "Jeremy Collier and the Politics of Theatrical Representation." In *Players, Playwrights, Playhouses: Investigating Performance, 1660-1800*, ed. Michael Cordner and Peter Holland, 135–51. Basingstoke: Palgrave Macmillan, 2007.

Frye, Northrop. *Anatomy of Criticism*. Princeton: Princeton University Press, 1951.

Fudge, Erica. *Perceiving Animals: Humans and Beasts in Early Modern English Culture*. Urbana and Chicago: University of Illinois Press, 2002.

———, Ruth Gilbert, and Susan Wiseman, ed. *At the Borders of the Human: Beasts, Bodies, and Natural Philosophy in the Early Modern Period*. Basingstoke, Palgrave Macmillan, 1999.

Fumerton, Patricia. *Unsettled: The Culture of Mobility and the Working Poor in Early Modern England*. Chicago: University of Chicago Press, 2006.

Ghosh, Amitav. *The Hungry Tide*. New York: Houghton Mifflin, 2005.

Goldstein, Philip. "Althusserian Theory: From Scientific Truth to Institutional History." Special issue, "The Legacy of Althusser," *Studies in 20th Century Literature* 18.1 (1994): 14–26.

Grady, Hugh. *Shakespeare, Machiavelli, and Montaigne: Power and Subjectivity from Richard II to Hamlet*. Oxford: Oxford University Press, 2002.

Grafton, Anthony. *Bring Out Your Dead: The Past as Revelation*. Cambridge: Harvard University Press, 2001.

Grafton, Anthony and Lisa Jardine. *From Humanism to the Humanities: Education and the Liberal Arts in Fifteenth- and Sixteenth-Century Europe*. London: Duckworth, 1986.

Graham, Jamey. "Consciousness, Self-Spectatorship, and Will to Power: Shakespeare's Stoic Conscience." *English Literary Renaissance* 44.2 (2014): 24–74.

Greenblatt, Stephen. "The Death of Hamnet and the Making of *Hamlet*." *The New York Review of Books*, Oct. 21, 2004. http://www.nybooks.com/articles/archives/2004/oct/21/the-death-of-hamnet-and-the-making-of-hamlet/.

———. "Shakespeare and the Exorcists." *Shakespearen Negotiations: The Circulation of Social Energy in Renaissance England*. Berkeley: University of California Press, 1988.

Greene, Robert. *Pandosto. The Triumph of Time*. In *Shakespeare's Library: A Collection of the Plays, Romances, Novels, Poems and Histories*, ed. William Hazlitt and John Collier. Vol. 4. London: Reeves and Turner, 1875.

Greimas, A.J. and Francis Rastier. "The Interaction of Semiotic Constraints." *Yale French Studies* 41 (1968): 86-105.

Guizot, Francois Pierre Guillame. *Shakespeare and His Times*. New York: Harper and Brothers, 1852.

Habenicht, Rudolph. "The Proverb Tradition in the Early Sixteenth-Century." In John Heywood, *A Dialogue of Proverbs*, ed. Rudolph Habenicht. Berkeley: University of California Press, 1963.

Haldeman, Joe. *The Forever War*. New York: St Martin's, 1974.

Halpern, Richard. *The Poetics of Primitive Accumulation: English Renaissance Culture and the Genealogy of Capital*. Cornell, NY: Cornell University Press, 1991.

Hamilton, W.D. "The Genetical Evolution of Social Behavior." *Journal of Theoretical Biology* 7 (1964): 1–52.

Harman, Graham. *Heidegger Explained: From Phenomenon to Thing*. Peru, Illinois: Open Court, 2007.

———. *Tool-Being: Heidegger and the Metaphysics of Objects*. Chicago: Open Court Press, 2002.

Harp, Richard. "Proverbs and Philosophy in *The Merchant of Venice* and *King Lear*." *Ben Jonson Journal* 16 (1995): 197–215.

Hayles, N. Katherine. *How We Became Posthuman: Virtual Bodies in Cybernetics, Literature and Informatics*. Chicago: University of Chicago Press, 1999.

Hegel, G.W.F. *Aesthetics: Lectures on Fine Art*. Vol. I. Ed. Hotho. Trans. T.M. Knox. 1973. https://www.marxists.org/reference/archive/hegel/works/ae/part2.htm.

"Henry VIII's Kitchens." *Historic Royal Palaces: Hampton Court Palace*. http://www.hrp.org.uk/HamptonCourtPalace/stories/thetudorkitchens.

Heywood, John. *A Dialogue of Proverbs*. 1546. Ed. Rudolph Habernicht. Oxford: University of Oxford Press, 1959.

Higgins, John. *Mirror for Magistrates*. 1574. In *King Lear*, ed. Vincent F. Petronella. Boston: Wadsworth, 2012.

Hirst, Derek. "Text, time, and the pursuit of 'British identities.'" In *British Identities and English Renaissance Literature*, ed. David Baker and Willy Maley. Cambridge: Cambridge University Press, 2002.

Hiscock, Andrew. *Reading Memory in Early Modern Literature*. Cambridge: Cambridge University Press, 2011.

Hiyama, Atsuki, Chiyo Nohara, Wataru Taira, Seira Kinjo, Masaki Iwata, and Joji M. Otaki. "The Fukushima Nuclear Accident and the Pale Grass Blue Butterfly: Evaluating Biological Effects of Long-term Low-dose Exposures." *BMC Evolutionary Biology* 13.168 (August 12, 2013). DOI: 10.1186/1471-2148-13-168. http://www.biomedcentral.com/1471-2148/13/168.

Hodder, Ian. *Entangled: An Archeology of the Relationships between Humans and Things*. Malden: Wiley Blackwell, 2012.

Holinshed, Raphael. *Chronicles of England, Scotland and Ireland*. 1577. In *King Lear*, ed. Vincent F. Petronella. Boston: Wadsworth, 2012.

Honeck, Robert P. *A Proverb in Mind: The Cognitive Science of Proverbial Wit and Wisdom.* London: Lawrence Erlbaum, 1997.

Hora, Stephen C., Detlof von Winterfeldt, and Kathleen M. Trauth. Expert Judgment on Inadvertent Human Intrusion into the Waste Isolation Pilot Plant. Sandia National Laboratories Report SAND90-3063 / UC-721, Dec. 1991. http://large.stanford.edu/courses/2011/ph241/dunn2/docs/SAND90-3063.pdf.

Houston, S.J. *James I.* 1973. London: Routledge, 2014.

Howard, Jean. "Renaissance Antitheatricality and the Politics of Gender and Rank in *Much Ado About Nothing.*" In *Shakespeare Reproduced: Text and History in Ideology,* ed. Jean Howard and Marion F. O'Connor. New York: Methuen, 1987.

Hulme, Peter. *Colonial Encounters: Europe and the Native Caribbean, 1492-1797.* London: Routledge, 1987.

Hyman, Wendy Beth, ed. *The Automaton in English Renaissance Literature.* Burlington: Ashgate, 2011. See esp. Brooke Conti's chapter, "The Mechanical Saint: Early Modern Devotion and the Language of Automation," 95–108.

Ignatieff, Michael. *The Needs of Strangers.* New York: Picador Macmillan, 2001.

"Issue Briefing: Impacts of Airplane Pollution on Climate Change and Health." *Flying Clean: Campaign to Cut Air Pollution.* http://www.flyingclean.com/impacts_airplane_pollution_climate_change_and_health.

Jameson, Fredric. *Brecht and Method.* New York: Verso, 1998.

———. *Postmodernism, or, The Cultural Logic of Late Capitalism.* Durham: Duke University Press, 1991. http://xroads.virginia.edu/~drbr/jameson/jameson.html.

Keefer, Michael H. "Accommodation and Synecdoche: Calvin's God in *King Lear.*" *Shakespeare Studies* 20 (1988): 147–68.

Kegl, Rosemary. *The Rhetoric of Concealment: Figuring Gender and Class in Renaissance Literature.* Ithaca: Cornell University Press, 1994.

King Leir. 1605. "Precursors of Shakespeare Plays." *Elizabethan Authors*. Transcribed by Barboura Flues. Ed. Robert Brazil. http://www.elizabethanauthors.org/king-leir-1605-1-16.htm.

Kott, Jan. *Shakespeare Our Contemporary*. New York: Methuen, 1965.

Laland, Kevin and Gillian Brown. *Sense and Nonsense: Evolutionary Perspectives on Human Behavior*. Oxford: Oxford University Press, 2002.

Latour, Bruno. *Pandora's Hope: Essays on the Reality of Science Studies*. Cambridge, MA: Harvard University Press, 1999.

Lodge, David. *Small World: An Academic Romance*. New York: Penguin, 1995.

Loewenstein, Joseph, ed. "Shakespeare and Skepticism." Special issue, *Shakespeare Quarterly Open Review*. http://shakespearequarterly.folger.edu/openreview/?page_id=4.

Lyly, John. *Euphues: The Anatomy of Wit*. 1578. In *John Lyly*, ed. John Dover Wilson. Cambridge: Macmillan and Bowes, 1905.

Mack, Maynard. *King Lear in Our Time*. Berkeley: University of California Press, 1972.

Madsen, Michael, dir. *Into Eternity: A Film for the Future*. Stockholm, Sweden: Atmo Media Network, 2010.

Marsden, Jean. "Female Spectatorship, Jeremy Collier and the Anti-Theatrical Debate." *ELH* 65 (1998): 877–98.

McCloskey, John. "The Emotive Use of Animal Imagery in *King Lear*." *Shakespeare Quarterly* 13.3 (1962): 321–25.

McNamara, Patrick and Martin Albert. "Neuropharmacology of Verbal Perseveration." *Seminars in Speech and Language* 25.4 (2004): 309–21. http://www.bu.edu/lab/files/2011/03/McNamara_Albert_2004.pdf.

Meillassoux, Quentin. *After Finitude: An Essay on the Necessity of Contingency*. Trans. Ray Brassier. London: Continuum Press, 2008.

Mentz, Steve. *At the Bottom of Shakespeare's Ocean*. London: Continuum, 2009.

———. "Strange weather in *King Lear*." *Shakespeare* 6.2: 139–52.

Mieder, Wolfgang. *The Politics of Proverbs: From Traditional Wisdom to Proverbial Stereotypes.* Madison: University of Wisconsin Press, 1997.

Miller, Clarence. "The Logic and Rhetoric of Proverbs in Erasmus' *Praise of Folly.*" In *Humanism and Style: Essay on Erasmus and More,* ed. Clarence Miller and Jerry Harp. Bethlehem, PA: Lehigh University Press, 2011.

Miner, Earl. "Stoic Reading in Renaissance English." *PMLA* 86 (1971): 1029–30.

Monmouth, Geoffrey. 1136. *History of the Kings of Britain.* Ed. Sebastian Evans. London: J.M. Dent, 1904.

Monsarrat, Gilles D. *Light from the Porch: Stoicism and English Renaissance Literature.* Paris: Didlier Erudition, 1984.

More, Thomas. *Utopia.* Ed. George Logan and Robert Adams. Cambridge: Cambridge University Press, 1975.

Moss, Ann. *Printed Commonplace-Books and the Structuring of Renaissance Thought.* Oxford: Oxford University Press, 1996.

Mousely, Andy. "Care, Scepticism and Speaking in the Plural: Posthumanisms and Humanisms in *King Lear.*" In *Posthumanist Shakespeares,* ed. Stefan Herbrechter and Ivan Callus, 97–113. London: Palgrave, 2012.

Nihon Sandai Jitsuroku [The True History of Three Reigns of Japan]. Ed. Sakamoto Taro. *The Six National Histories of Japan.* (UBC Press: Tokyo, 1991), 169-186.

Pacchioli, David. "How Is Fukushima's Fallout Affecting Marine Life?" *Oceanus Magazine,* May 2, 2013. http://www.whoi.edu/oceanus/feature/how-is-fukushimas-fallout-affecting-marine-life.

Paster, Gail Kern. *Humoring the Body: Emotions and the Shakespearean Stage.* Chicago: University of Chicago Press, 2004.

Patterson, Annabel. *Fables of Power: Aesopian Writing and Political History.* Durham: Duke University Press, 1991.

"Permanent Markers Implementation Plan." August 19, 2004. http://www.wipp.energy.gov/library/PermanentMarkersImplementationPlan.pdf.

Perry, Curtis. *The Making of Jacobean Culture: James I and the Renegotiation of Elizabethan Literary Practice*. Cambridge: Cambridge University Press, 1997.

Phillips, Margaret Mann. *The 'Adages' of Erasmus: A Study with Translations*. Cambridge: Cambridge University Press, 1964.

Popper, Karl. *Knowledge and the Body-Mind Problem: In Defense of Interaction*. Ed. M.A. Notturno. London: Routledge, 1994.

Pugliatti, Paola. *Beggary and Theatre in Early Modern England*. Burlington: Ashgate, 2003.

Raber, Karen. *Animal Bodies, Renaissance Culture*. Philadelphia: University of Pennsylvania Press, 2013.

Rancière, Jacques. *The Emancipated Spectator*. London: Verso, 2011.

Reynolds, Bryan. *Transversal Enterprises in the Drama of Shakespeare and his Contemporaries: Fugitive Explorations*. New York: Palgrave, 2006.

Rilke, Rainer Maria. *Duino Elegies*. Portland: Tavern Books, 2013. Reprint.

Schalkwyk, David. "Text and Performance, Reiterated: A Reproof Valiant or Lie Direct?" *Shakespearean International Yearbook* 10 (2010): 47–76.

Schorr-Kon, Sophia. *Delphine's Call. Sophia Schorr-Kon*. http://www.sophiaschorr-kon.com.

Shakespeare, William. *Hamlet*. Ed. Stephen Greenblatt, Walter Cohen, Jean E. Howard, and Katharine Eisaman Maus. *The Norton Shakespeare: Based on the Oxford Edition*. 2nd edn. London: Norton, 2008.

———. *Henry IV Part I*. Ed. Stephen Greenblatt, Walter Cohen, Jean E. Howard, and Katharine Eisaman Maus. *The Norton Shakespeare: Based on the Oxford Edition*. 2nd edn. London: Norton, 2008.

———. *Henry V*. Ed. Stephen Greenblatt, Walter Cohen, Jean E. Howard, and Katharine Eisaman Maus. *The Norton Shakespeare: Based on the Oxford Edition*. 2nd edn. London: Norton, 2008.

———. *Macbeth*. Ed. Stephen Greenblatt, Walter Cohen, Jean E. Howard, and Katharine Eisaman Maus. *The Norton Shake-*

speare: Based on the Oxford Edition. 2nd edn. London: Norton, 2008.

———. *King Lear.* The Conflated Text. Ed. Stephen Greenblatt, Walter Cohen, Jean E. Howard, and Katharine Eisaman Maus. *The Norton Shakespeare: Based on the Oxford Edition*. 2nd edn. London: Norton, 2008.

———. *A Midsummer Night's Dream*. Ed. Stephen Greenblatt, Walter Cohen, Jean E. Howard, and Katharine Eisaman Maus. *The Norton Shakespeare: Based on the Oxford Edition*. 2nd edn. London: Norton, 2008.

Shalhoub-Kevorkian, Nadera. "Voice Therapy for Women Aligned with Political Prisoners: A Case Study of Trauma among Palestinian Women in the Second Intifada." *Social Service Review* 79.2 (2005): 322–43.

Shannon, Laurie. *The Accommodated Animal: Cosmopolity in Shakespearean Locales*. Chicago: University of Chicago Press, 2013.

Sheehan, Bernard. *Savagism and Civility: Indians and Englishmen in Colonial Virginia*. Cambridge: Cambridge University Press, 1980.

Shklovsky, Victor. "Art as Technique." In *The Critical Tradition: Classic Texts and Contemporary Trends,* ed. David H. Richter. New York: Bedford, 2006.

Sidney, Philip. *Arcadia*. 1590. In *King Lear,* ed. Vincent F. Petronella.Boston: Wadsworth, 2012.

Silverstone, Catherine. *Shakespeare, Trauma and Contemporary Performance*. London: Routledge, 2011.

Simon, L., J. Greenberg, and J. Brehm. "Trivialization: The Forgotten Mode of Dissonance Reduction." *Journal of Personality and Social Psychology* 68 (1960): 247–60.

Snyders, Frans. *The Pantry*. Ca. 1620. Location unknown. *Wikimedia Commons*. https://commons.wikimedia.org/wiki/File:Frans_SNYDERS,_The_Pantry.JPG.

Stalder, Daniel. "The Power of Proverbs: Dissonance Reduction through Common Sayings." *Current Research in Social Psychology* 15.7 (2010): 1–10. http://citeseerx.ist.psu.edu/viewdoc/download?doi=10.1.1.409.8358&rep=rep1&type=pdf.

———— and P.G. Devine. "Why Does Social Comparison Reduce Dissonance?" *Journal of Social and Personal Relationships* 29.3 (2012): 302–23.

Stone, Lawrence. *The Crisis of the Aristocracy, 1558-1641*. Oxford: Oxford University Press, 1965.

Strier, Richard. *Unrepentant Renaissance: From Petrarch to Shakespeare to Milton*. Chicago: University of Chicago Press, 2011.

Stuurman, Siep. "Herodotus and Sima Qian: History and the Anthropological Turn in Ancient Greece and Han China." *Journal of World History* 19.1 (2008): 1–40.

Taro, Sakamoto. *The Six National Histories of Japan*. UBC Press: Tokyo, 1991.

Taylor, George Coffin. "Shakespeare's Use of the Idea of the Beast in Man." *Studies in Philology* 42.3 (1945): 530–43.

Thomas, Keith. *Religion and the Decline of Magic*. London: Penguin, 2013.

Tilley, Christopher. *The Materiality of Stone: Explorations in Landscape Phenomenology*. Oxford: Berg Publishers, 2004.

Tilley, Morris. *A Dictionary of Proverbs in England in the Sixteenth and Seventeenth Century*. Ann Arbor: University of Michigan Press, 1950.

Trivers, Robert L. "The Evolution of Reciprocal Altruism." *The Quarterly Review of Biology* 46.1 (1971): 35–57.

Veblen, Thorstein. *The Theory of the Leisure Class*. 1899. New Brunswick: Transaction Publishers, 1992.

Vignemont, Frederique and Tania Singer. "The Empathic Brain: How, When and Why?" *Trends in Cognitive Sciences* 10.10 (2006): 435–41.

Vince, Gaia. *Adventures in the Anthropocene: A Journey to the Heart of the Planet We Made*. London: Chatto and Windus, 2014.

Vives, Juan Luis. "Of the Mind." In *An Introduction to Widsom*, trans. Sir Richard Moryson. 1540. In *Vives: On Education: A Translation of the* De Tradendis Disciplinis *of Juan Luis Vives*, ed. and trans. by Foster Watson. Cambridge: Cambridge University Press, 1913.

Whitcrosse, Julian. "Finland's Brilliant Plan for Dealing with Nuclear Waste: Pulling a Keyser Söze." *io9*, May 13, 2012. http://io9.com/5909853/finlands-brilliant-plan-for-dealing-with-nuclear-waste-pulling-a-kaiser-soze.

Willacy, Mark. *Fukushima and the Inside Story of the Nuclear Meltdowns*. Sydney: Macmillan Australia, 2013.

Williams, Raymond. *The Country and the City*. London: Chatto and Windus, 1973.

Wilson, F.P. "The Proverbial Wisdom of Shakespeare." In *Shakespearean and Other Studies*. Oxford: Oxford University Press, 1969.

Wood, Michael. *Shakespeare*. New York: Basic Books, 2003.

Woodbridge, Linda. *Vagrancy, Homelessness, and English Renaissance Literature*. Chicago: University of Illinois Press, 2001.

Worthen. William. *Shakespeare and the Force of Modern Performance*. Cambridge: Cambridge University Press, 2003.

Yachnin, Paul A. "Sheepishness in *The Winter's Tale*." In *How to Do Things with Shakespeare*, ed. Laurie Maguire, 210–29. Oxford and Malden, MA: Blackwell Publishing, 2008.

Yates, Julian. "Accidental Shakespeare." *Shakespeare Studies* 34 (2006): 90–122.

———. "Counting Sheep: Dolly Does Utopia (Again)." *Rhizomes* 8 (Spring 2004). http://www.rhizomes.net/issue8/yates2.htm.

———. *Error, Misuse, Failure: Object Lessons From The English Renaissance*. Minneapolis: University of Minnesota Press, 2003.

———. "Humanist Habitats, or 'Eating Well' with Thomas More's *Utopia*." In *Environment and Embodiment in Early Modern England*, ed. Mary Floyd Wilson and Garrett A. Sullivan, Jr., 187–209. New York: Palgrave, 2007.

———. "Shakespeare's Kitchen Archives." In *Speculative Medievalisms: Discography*, ed. The Petropunk Collective [Eileen Joy, Anna Klosowska, Nicola Masciandaro, and Michael O'Rourke], 179–200. Brooklyn: punctum books, 2013.

Zylinska, Joanna. *Minimal Ethics for the Anthropocene.* Ann Arbor: Open Humanities Press, 2014.

INDEX

Z

Made in the USA
Charleston, SC
11 November 2016